with BOMPAS & PARR

TUTTI FRUTTI

and Friends

Published by Bompas & Parr Editions

HARVEST
OF THE

Fields,
Orchards
& Jungles

FRUIT ESSAYS
& INSIGHTS

06

FRUIT

A JOURNEY TO
THE CENTRE
OF THE BOWL

SALADS

32

EAT DRINK AND BE MERRY FOR TOMORROW WE DIET!

ICES,
JELLIES &
TRIFLE

52

BAKING &
PRESERVING
ADDRESSING THE
ALVINE NEED

#005

66

74

82

96

100

Introduction

By Bompas & Parr
Photography by Nathan Pask

Across the globe there are 240,000 to 500,000 plant species that bear fruits of which 70,000 to 80,000 are thought to be edible and tasty. How many have you tried? Have you carved into ultra-exotic, pungent and forbidden fruits like the durian, tarap, bullock's heart, atemoya, pitabu and cainito? With some determination and a willingness to venture into Chinese supermarkets, night markets and the living jungles of the world you can feast like a hero.

At Bompas & Parr we are obsessed with fruit. From the mysteries of the mouth numbing snake fruit to *Pollia condensata*, the shiniest living thing known to mankind, we've been diligently studying the world's greatest fruits.

This research has taken in exotics such as the cauliflorous jabuticaba, the eerily flavoured durian (so pungent it is banned on public transport in many Asian countries,) and *Monstera deliciosa* described on the Barbican's plant plaque thus:

'*M. deliciosa* is usually cultivated as an ornamental house plant, but is sometimes grown for its unusual edible fruit. When mature it carries 6–8 inch creamy arum-like spathes followed by green cone-shaped fruits. Which when fully ripe taste like mixed fruit salad.'

Our work has also covered seemingly mundane fruits. Tracking down lost flavours of Surinam cherries or neglected varieties of the pineapple – a fruit once considered so magnificent in England that Regency hostesses would rent them by the night to impress dinner party guests.

Even the common banana has a racy past. In living memory it was seen as an exotic fruit. At the end of WWII every child in Britain was allotted a banana. For Evelyn Waugh's children the great day was particularly memorable. They had been counting down the hours to the exciting arrival of the banana ration. Auberon Waugh tells the sorry tale in *Will This Do?* Their expectations were soon crushed: the bananas 'were put on my father's plate, and before the anguished eyes of his children, he poured on cream, which was almost unprocurable, and sugar, which was heavily rationed, and ate all three … He was permanently marked down in my estimation from that moment on, in a way which no amount of sexual transgression would have achieved.'

Being invited to present a fruit-centric installation for Kew Gardens across the summer of 2013 was being thrown in the briar patch. We thought it would be best to explore fruit salad, the flavour sensation that occurs when many fruits collide in the bowl. Tutti Frutti was born, a vast fruit salad boating lake at Kew with a pineapple island, hidden banana grotto and an art installation from Mileece, which allows real communication with fruiting plants.

Rather than write a conventional exhibition guide for the installation we thought it would be far more exciting to work with friends, lovers, mentors, culinary heroes and our artistic inspirations to explore the gustatory implications of fruit salad. You are reading the fresh and varied results. The book in your hands takes already surprising fruits into unusual realms, documenting the geometry of fruit, tasseomancy, the intriguing Pulfrich effect, embalming, blue as the international colour of raspberries and a host of tasty and luxurious fruit based dishes.

Through countless recipes, tales and photography we want to look again at the fruit on the end of our spoon or in our glass when pomology (the study of fruit) and mixology aligns. So welcome, come read the fruit secrets of some of the greatest creative minds of our generation, the zenith of gustatory creativity. Let this be the beginning of your own fruit-based adventure, an odyssey to taste whole constellations of fruits and unite them in a single bowl. Let's get fruity!

HARVEST OF THE

Fields, Orchards & Jungles

FRUIT ESSAYS & INSIGHTS

Spaces of Banana Control:
A Field Trip to the Exotic Ripening Rooms of The Bronx

By Nicola Twilley of Edible Geography

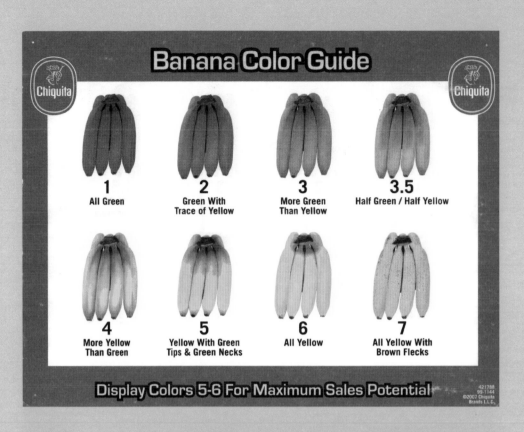

Above: Consult the banana colour guide for maximum sales potential
Below: Atmospheric design – The Easy Ripe generator produces a safe, even flow
of the potentially explosive ethelyne, helping the fruit to ripen

In 1944, the 'First Lady of Fruit', Miss Chiquita, sashayed onto movie screens and banana stickers across America. Wearing a 'Tutti-Frutti' hat inspired by Carmen Miranda, a flamenco skirt, and what appear to be false eyelashes, this sexy banana lady disembarked from her white steamship and sang a jingle that helped a generation treat tropical fruit right:

'I'm a Chiquita banana and I've come to say / Bananas have to ripen in a certain way / [...] Bananas like the climate of the very, very tropical equator / So you should never put bananas in the refrigerator.'

However, contrary to popular belief, as well as to Miss Chiquita's charming lyrics, bananas are the ultimate refrigerated fruit. Before refrigeration, bananas were an exotic curiosity, equivalent to the Southeast Asian langsat or the Andean cherimoya today; now, they are the most consumed fruit in both Britain and the US, forcing the more traditional apple into second place.

Although the oldest banana skin found in the UK dates to Tudor times, until Fyffes introduced the first refrigerated banana boat in 1901, with the American company United Fruit (which later became Chiquita) following swiftly behind in 1903, most Britons and Americans would never have even seen a banana, let alone eaten one. Indeed, an 1899 article about bananas in *Scientific American* included careful instructions, seemingly written by someone who was not personally familiar with the art of peeling a banana, on what to do should their readers encounter this peculiar looking fruit: 'The fruit is peeled by splitting the skin longitudinally and giving it a rotary motion with the hands'.

Of course, given its phallic shape, ladies lucky enough to be offered the tropical rarity were advised to consume it using a knife and fork, and, indeed, without the preservative powers of refrigeration, bananas would have arrived in Liverpool or New York far too overripe and squishy, if not completely liquefied, to be eaten out of hand.

In order to become a global commodity rather than a curious, mushy tropical treat, the banana has to be harvested completely unripe and transported in a state of cryogenic suspended animation. Bananas are cut while green, hard and immature, washed in cool water (both to begin removing field heat and to stop them from leaking their natural latex), and then held at 13°C – originally in a refrigerated steamship, painted white to reflect the sun, today, in a refrigerated container – until they reach their country of consumption weeks later.

What this means is that ripening must then be artificially induced, in a specialised architecture of pressurized, temperature- and atmosphere-controlled rooms that fool the banana into thinking it is still back on the plant in tropical Ecuador. While Europe's largest banana ripening complex can be found in a business park outside Coventry, efficiently turning ten million green bananas yellow each week, New York City's supermarkets, grocers, coffee shops and food cart vendors are served by just a handful of banana ripening outfits — one in Brooklyn, one in Long Island and a small facility inside the main Hunt's Point Terminal Market, and my field trip destination: Banana Distributors of New York, in the Bronx.

When Paul Rosenblatt answers the phone, he says 'Bananas!' Rosenblatt ships a million boxes of bananas every year from the Banana Distributors of New York facility on Drake Street, in the Hunt's Point section of the Bronx. On a grey Thursday in

October, when I visited for a behind-the-scenes tour of the banana supply chain's evolving architecture of atmospheric control, he had 20,000 cases of bananas, each weighing 18kg and containing roughly 100 individual fingers, in the building.

Rosenblatt told me that he aims to ripen fruit in five days at 16.6°C, but, in order to schedule fruit readiness in accordance with supply and demand, he can push a room in four days at 17.7°C, or extend the process to seven days at 14.4°C.

'The energy coming off a box of ripening bananas could heat a small apartment,' Rosenblatt explained, which means that heavy-duty refrigeration is required to keep each room temperature controlled to within a half a degree.

To add to the complexity, customers can choose from different degrees of ripeness, ranging from 1 (all green) to 7 (all yellow with brown sugar spots). Up on the wall, Rosenblatt has several Banana Colour Guides, originally developed by the industry to help standardise banana maturity ratings and first published in 1950 by Harry Von Loesecke of the United Fruit Company in the industry bible, *Bananas: Chemistry, Physiology, Technology.* Von Loesecke sneaks in a category 8 banana in his colour plate illustration, but it is more brown than yellow and would never be offered for sale today.

Banana Distributors of New York proudly promise that they have 'Every Color, Every Day', although Rosenblatt gets nervous if he has more than 2,000 boxes of any particular shade. To provide this variety, a banana ripening facility has to have a minimum of five or six rooms (Banana Distributors of New York has twenty-two). Each room holds between 1,000 and 2,000 boxes, which means that a banana distributor has to move at least 5,000 boxes each week to make the business worthwhile. This, Rosenblatt explains, has squeezed out the two dozen smaller, three- or four-room operators that used to be sprinkled around New York City in the 1970s.

The most popular wholesale shades are between 2.5 and 3.5, but much depends on the retailer's size and target market. The supermarket chain Fairway, which sources its bananas from Banana Distributors of New York, expects to hold bananas for a couple of days, and will therefore buy greener bananas than a smaller corner shop that turns its stock over on a daily basis. 'Street vendors,' Rosenblatt notes, as well as shops serving a mostly Latin American customer base, 'like full yellow', although Chiquita's market research shows that the US population in general tends to prefer 5s (yellow with green tips). Personally, he eats only a couple of bananas each week, and favours fully ripe 'sevens'.

In addition to precise temperature control, the ripening process also depends on atmospheric design. Over a 24-hour period, each roomful of bananas is gassed with ethylene, a plant hormone that accelerates ripening (and is also, curiously, the most produced organic compound in the world). When Rosenblatt opened the door on a recently gassed room, the smell was revolting — like a beer-soaked pub carpet, the morning after.

The ethylene is produced in a low, even flow from portable 'Easy-ripe' generators. In the past, Rosenblatt explained, rooms would be injected with a burst of ethylene released from a cylinder, which not only made it much harder to achieve an even distribution among the stacked bananas, but also posed a heightened fire risk — ethylene is highly flammable, and in the early days of injection technology, fatal banana ripening room explosions were not uncommon.

Newspaper archives are treasure troves of this kind of banana-related tragedy, from the 1936 ripening room explosion at the Pittsburgh Banana Company, which destroyed church bell towers across the street, to a 1950 explosion at the Committee of Direction of Fruit Marketing ripening chambers in Brisbane, Australia, during which an unlucky worker was 'hurled into a brick wall and covered by hundreds of pounds of hard green bananas'. The best-known story in the trade involves an exploding fruit truck in northern Japan, which sent seven tons of bananas sailing through the air, injuring several bystanders.

For banana-ripening enthusiasts, a visit to the Banana Distributors of New York is particularly exciting because original pressurised rooms from the late 1970s are still in use, alongside state-of-the-art Dutch door technology. The older rooms are a legacy of the pre-pallet era, when bananas used to arrive loose and were carefully stacked from concrete floor to ceiling 'like bricks' packed tight and fan-ventilated to force air around each hand.

Using these old rooms to ripen today's boxed bananas requires a few adaptations: eight-box stacks are covered with a tarp to create a vacuum, and three axial fans draw air through the carefully measured corridors in between. Even and efficient air circulation is critical to successful temperature control and ethylene distribution, as is occasional venting, as the ripening bananas consume oxygen and release carbon dioxide.

'With bananas,' according to Rosenblatt, 'it's all about ventilation.'

The next rooms that Rosenblatt showed me are, he mentioned almost as an aside, the first two-tier banana ripening rooms ever built. In 1988, he explained, 'this guy called Jim Still came along and offered to build them for free, as an experiment.' They worked, and Jim Still is now known as Banana Jim™, founder and president of ripening industry leaders, Global Logic, LLC.

In these double-decker ripening rooms, the fans hang on the ceiling, so that air is forced, rather than drawn, through, allowing for even more uniform ripening. In addition, to increased capacity and improved ripening uniformity, these vertical air-flow banana chambers can be loaded and unloaded using fork-lift trucks in 20 minutes or less.

With minor improvements in fan engineering, and the optional addition of a third tier, brand-new banana ripening rooms still look identical to today. 'Nowadays, all the technological innovation,' Rosenblatt tells me, 'is to be found in doors.' He points out some old-school, roll-up airtight doors, explaining that 'we call these widowmakers – we never stand under them.'

I asked Rosenblatt about new, in-container ripening systems, which threaten to make the banana ripening room extinct by integrating the process into the final few days of a banana's boat journey, so that it can be unloaded from a freighter and trucked straight to the supermarket. 'Banana Jim' still has actually filed a patent for his Ripe-Anywhere™ container system, and promotes it under the humble tagline, 'It was a modest invention … but it changed a planet'.

"The energy coming off a box of ripening bananas could heat a small apartment,"
Paul Rosenblatt, Banana Distributors of New York

Rosenblatt is not convinced: 'Walmart could do containers, but in New York City, retailers don't have the volume'. Nonetheless, the future of his family business is uncertain. While his father-in-law got his start in the fruit trade at the age of eight, working for street pedlars, Rosenblatt told me that he hopes his own children don't go into banana ripening.

The hours are certainly unappealing: Banana Distributors is open from 10pm to noon, every night. To the downsides, I added my own mistrust of banana boxes, dating back to a scarring experience with a large, furry spider as a 16-year-old shelf stacker at Waitrose. At Fyffes' massive Coventry ripening facility, staff in the sorting room report unpleasant encounters with a lizard and two tarantulas. Rosenblatt told me that in his 39 years in the banana trade, he has never seen a snake or lizard, and has only come across one spider, which he gave to the Bronx Zoo.

I said goodbye as the final trailer was being loaded and shipped out for the day. Nearly two million bananas pass through these ripening rooms on their journey to New York consumers each week – a vital link in the largely invisible, highly specialised architecture of artificial refrigeration that has enabled the banana to become and remain our favourite fruit.

NOTE: This essay is adapted from an earlier blog post at www.ediblegeography.com

The Geometry of Plants

by Anna Murray of Patternity

Patterns are something you come across every day. They are everywhere you go and in everything you do. The closer you look at the fascinating and infinite world of pattern the deeper you can hope to understand the wonders of world and all that's in it. But where to begin? Perhaps the best place to start this daunting voyage of discovery is to take a look at some of the patterns in the natural world. Zooming in even closer for examination of the mysterious geometry of plants...

Looking around, you might imagine that the branches and leaves are arranged at random, haphazardly. The reality is, however, that the points at which every branch, leaf, stem, bud or seed emerge, have all been set out with fixed laws and miraculous measures. Despite the astonishing smorgasbord of the many different flora and fauna that surround us many have creepily closely comparable features whether viewed under the microscope or from afar. Take for example – the Romanesco broccoli – such refined regularity in nature was, and in many cases still is, taken as evidence of God's guiding hand. And understandably – for most observers ruminating for any length at its beautifully orchestrated florets, its fractal spiralling and tactful repeated twirling is mesmerising.

'God sleeps in the minerals, awakens in plants, walks in animals, and thinks in man.'
— Arthur Young (RainyQuote.com, 10 May, 2013)

Like staring up at the night's sky, delving into the world of pattern in plants can be humbling and with resounding results – sparking philosophical ruminations on life, death and the universe. Our logical reasoning of the man-made world informs us that 'making a pattern requires a patterner'. When we construct an architectural pattern, it is through considered planning and execution, with each individual element carefully laid in place. Our experience from human technologies only goes so far in explaining nature's creation – questions duly arise, 'surely there must be a master at work? What ho' this higher helping hand?! Which creative genius would have such patience to concoct such a magnificent form? And more fundamentally... why?!'

And this questioning could all begin at the local grocery shop. As the naturalist Joseph Banks once mused over patterns found in nature 'Compared to this, what are the Cathedrals or palaces built by men! Mere models or play things, as diminutive as his works will always be when compared with those of nature. What now is the boast of the architect! Regularity, the only part in which he fancied himself to exceed his mistress, Nature, is here found in her possession, and here it has been for ages undescribed.'

So back down here on earth, how can we systematically dig beneath the surface of this mysterious world of natural growth and form? The answer it would appear lies with some simple, and very fundamental mathematics. So, if pattern comes from the Latin *pater*, meaning father, while the word 'matter' derives from the Latin *mater*, meaning mother who exactly is the daddy? And how on earth do we find him...? Perhaps we need a paternity test...

Setting off on our geometrical expedition in search of our natural father zooms us straight back in time to 13th century Italy, to Italian mathematician, Leonardo of Pisa who was more famously known as 'Fibonacci'. Fibonacci AKA the poster boy of the numerical system famously drew a new and excited audience to the wonders of mathematics with his weighty 600 page, handwritten (ouch!) compendium in which he cited a sequence so simple it's almost baffling. Here each number is created by adding together the previous two – starting 1 1 2 3 5 8 13 21 – a pattern that continues to infinity. The search for an explanation of the persistent occurrence of Fibonacci's numbers in nature has gone on for over three centuries – and the sequence occurs so frequently in nature that although not impossible it's a challenge to find a plant or fruit structure that does not conform to it. The skin of the pineapple is a good example of Fibonacci in nature. It is arranged as two interlocking helices, eight in one direction, thirteen in the other, each being a Fibonacci number.

Venturing forth, as the ratios between consecutive numbers get progressively closer to a single number, 1.618034 (to the first six decimal places) it would be impossible to go any further before next encountering the almighty Golden Ratio – a number so imbedded into the fabric of the universe that it has haunted human culture for thousands of years. Some of the greatest mathematical minds of all ages have spent endless hours over this simple ratio and its so-called mystical properties. 'Where there is matter, there is geometry,' said Johannes Kepler, but the fascination is not confined just to mathematicians. Biologists, artists, musicians, historians, architects, psychologists, and even mystics have pondered and debated the basis of its ubiquity and appeal. Also known as the divine section it has long been considered to have near mystical properties – even so far as being entwined with our DNA. The figure is supposed to represent an 'ideal' proportion that many people instinctively prefer and has been used often for the proportions of classical architecture – the Parthenon is proportioned this way. Even the ratios of our own body's natural geometry conforms to the Golden Ratio.

So does any of this actually matter? Why should we even care? Musing more deeply about what's growing in our garden or sitting on the end of our fork can have small but powerful results. As philosopher Bertrand Russell puts it well, 'Mathematics, rightly viewed, possesses not only truth, but supreme beauty – a beauty cold and austere, like that of sculpture, without appeal to any part of our weaker nature, without the gorgeous trappings of painting or music, yet sublimely pure, and capable of a stern perfection such as only the greatest art can show'.

An awareness of these fascinating numerical sequences has the power to elevate contemplation of the mundane operations of the Brussels sprout to magnificent musings on matter and the universe. Through understanding pattern we can begin to dig a little deeper into the inner workings of the cosmos – a powerful tool for learning that can drive forward our man-made designs and innovations – much can be learned from the inner workings of the natural world.

Here's how artist and designer Bruno Munari sees it, 'Copying nature is one thing and understanding nature is another. Copying nature can be simply a form of manual dexterity that does not help us to understand, for it shows us things just as we are accustomed to seeing them. But studying the structures of nature, observing the evolution of forms, can give everyone a better understanding of the world we live in.'

Pattern is a universal language that connects us all – it shapes the world around us. Understanding more about how spontaneous pattern formation occurs has the power to unite many disparate fields – from science to sociology, architecture to anthropology, music to mechanics, engineering to environmentalism... and beyond. Most importantly, being more aware of the world around us, and our collective patterns and interconnectivity can generate a good dose of empathy. Being more aware of pattern can remind us that we are all part of a greater whole, perhaps positively shaping the way we engage with our environment and each other.

This can have a profound effect. Iain McGilchrist, psychiatrist, doctor and author gives a clear insight, 'The kind of attention we bring to bear on the world changes the nature of the world, we attend to, the very nature of the world in which those functions would be carried out, and in which those things would exist. Attention changes what kind of thing comes into being for us, in that way it changes the world'.

The voyage of discovery is by no means over...

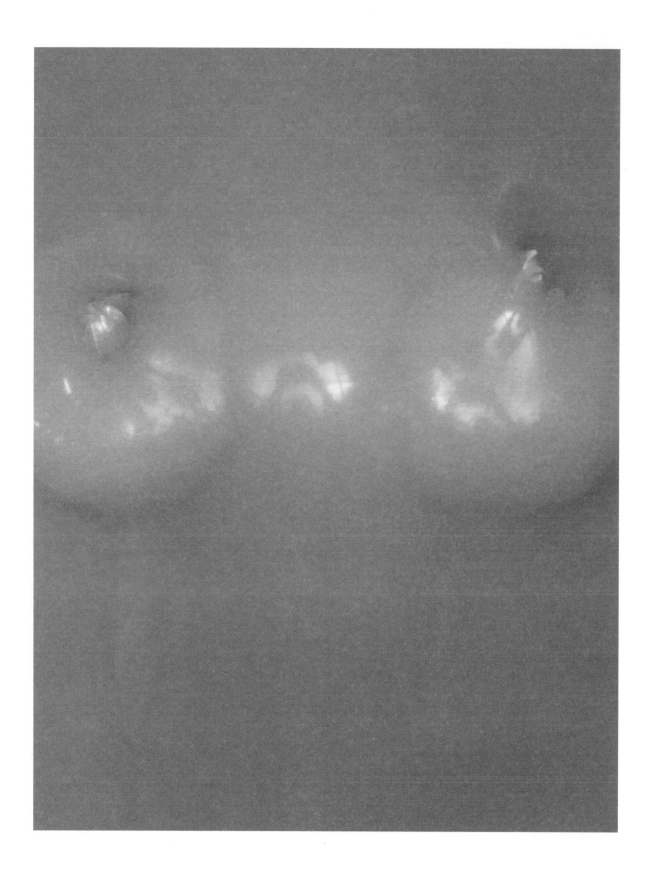

Rude Fruit
Photography: Katy Pople. Art direction: Emma Rios and Olivia French

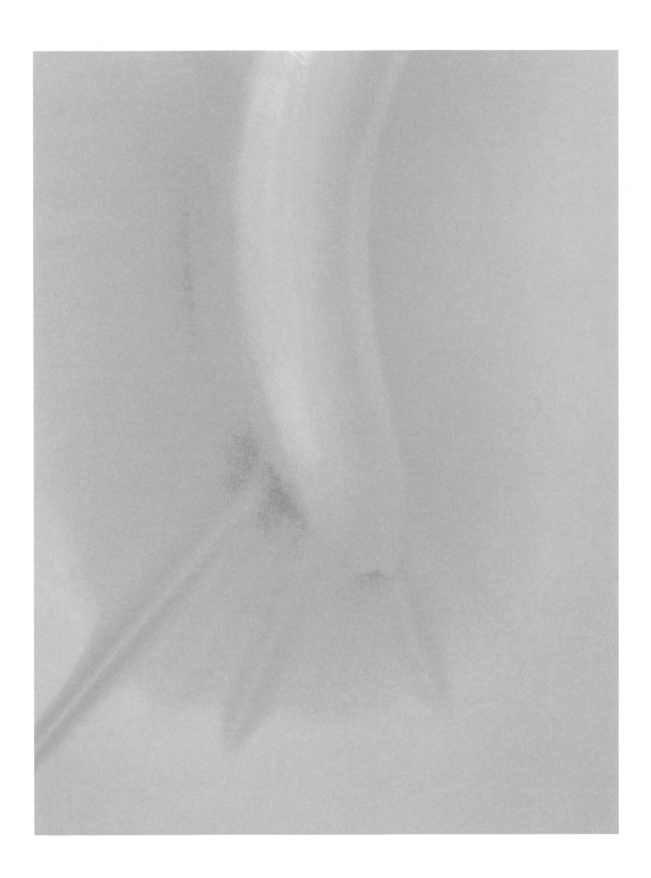

Raspberries are Blue

By Sam Jacob of FAT

There's a version of the world arranged in newsagents' sweet jars, frozen in tubes of ice pop, bottled in aluminium cans and packed on supermarket isles. It's a low resolution version of our world, where shapes, colours and tastes of nature are approximated as closely as chemistry and food regulations allow. However blocky and simplified this confectionery world is, there remains a direct relationship between the synthetic and the natural, between the sign and the signified. Take colour. Red is strawberry, orange is orange, yellow equals banana or lemon, green equals lime, purple equals blackcurrant and so on.

Colour acts like packaging, like a sign visually signifying the products' flavour on the supermarket shelf. It acts too as a synaesthetic cue to our taste buds, physiologically nudging us to taste in the right way. Artificial colouring first tells us what something is and then helps us believe in the veracity of an artificial colour's flavour.

Artificial raspberry colour once followed this model. An extract of coal tar called amaranth (AKA E123 or FD&C Red No. 2) was used to give foods a dark raspberry red. But in 1976, E123 was classified 'Very Dangerous' by the Food Standards Agency and withdrawn from the market. And into this void steps, for reasons we will speculate on later, Brilliant Blue FCF (Blue 1), or, as it appears on your packaging, E133. Or, to give it it's chemical name C37H34N2Na2O9S3; chemically synthesised from aromatic hydrocarbons derived from petroleum.

(As an aside, if you think this is somewhat undigestible, you'll be tickled to know that artificial raspberry flavour listed on a product's ingredients as 'natural flavouring', is actually an exudate from the anal glands of the mature North American and European Beaver.)

Raspberry's Brilliant Blue FCF strikes a lightening bolt through the simple call and response of synthetic fruit colourings. It's a bright blue anomaly where the fruit and its artificial representation diverge completely. We can speculate that the reasons run something like this. There are only so many artificial food colours that are safe to eat. At the moment FD&C Red No. 2 was banned there were simply no reds free that weren't already used to signify other red fruit. Think of the congestion of radio frequencies, where it becomes impossible to broadcast on a particular wavelength because of the interference it would cause to its neighbours. In the spectrum of artificial fruit colours, red was already congested with strawberry, cherry and so on but the non-natural palette was, given the prevailing desire for colours to mimic nature, free.

Perhaps this radio analogy is more literal that it first seems: colours are frequencies too and in the world of artificial confectionery, they broadcast the idea of the fruit they represent.

But blue? Why would raspberry suddenly become blue? First, we could look at nature for its origins. If you look hard at a raspberry, you can see a blue tinge to the red, a kind of purple shadow of blue + red. And there is a Blue Raspberry, *Rubus leucodermis* but let's face it, it's not blue like artificial raspberry blue. If we were painting a still life, we'd be at the wilder end of representation before we found ourselves breaking out a tube of bright blue for the raspberries. We'd be Impressionist perhaps, Cubist maybe. And like these early forms of abstraction, we're certainly at the point where painting diverges from the need to imitate nature, at the moment art becomes concerned with abstract and the conceptual acts, with the depiction of interior psychology rather than the visual world, where art becomes concerned with perception and sensation in and of themselves.

Raspberry's blueness has little to do with the fruit it represents. Instead it's blue as a thing itself, and like all colours, it has its own histories, cultures and meanings. Art historically speaking, blue was a difficult colour to create. It first came from lapis lazuli, the semi-precious stone mined in Afghanistan and exported across the ancient world. The expense and exoticness gave blues a special status that later meant it became the signature the colour of the Virgin Mary's clothes, then of royalty.

In modern art, blue retains aspects of this specialness. We could think of Picasso's blue period, or Yves Klein's International Blue, or of Derek Jarman's final film *Blue* that consists of a single shot of saturated blue filling the screen. Jarman's blue was like the signature signal of the screen exposed, like the iridescent Videodrome glow that emanates from TV's in darkened rooms, flickering across the faces of its viewers.

We could think of other blues: The Blues, Blue Monday, electric blue, blue movies, blue sky thinking, the great blue yonder. These blues are imaginative states rather than things, abstract ideas not representations. Blue, then is a colour of otherness, of technological newness, of a state beyond the normal world.

Truth, difficult enough a concept at the best of times, is an especially troubling concept when it comes to food. We lurch from one crisis to another that stem from the sheer complexity of agribusiness, from the scale and intricate global logistics of farming and food processing. One could argue that it's in supermarket aisles where we are really confronted with the problem of the natural in a contemporary world, where cultural ideas of naturalness intersect violently with economic and technological realties. More than this, we might contend that this is where the ideas of nature are manufactured.

Against this effort to naturalise the unnatural world of food production, raspberry's blue revels in its artificiality, refusing to imitate nature. In this way, raspberry blue has a truth that imitative synthetic colours mask. It suggests an order of synthetic foods set free not only from the natural world but also from the need to present themselves – however unnatural they may be – as 'natural'.

Blue is a colour of technology, of exception and otherness and it's perhaps these narratives that we bite into with a Brilliant Blue FCF Mr Freeze. Maybe raspberry blue is the shock troop of another food spectrum, marking our turn away from nostalgic images of farming that haunt our culinary imagination. E133 suggests that food no longer comes from the field but from the lab, something synthesised rather than reared. It suggests that the things we eat might become abstract notions: the taste of wavelengths, rather than biology, where we might lick across the spectrum into infrareds and ultraviolets that we can hardly yet imagine.

Top Fruit in History

By Beth Adams of Bompas & Parr
Illustrations from the Kew Archives

Illustrations reproduced with the kind permission of the Director
and the Board of Trustees, Royal Botanic Gardens, Kew

Coconut

Botanical name: *Cocos nucifera.* Family: Arecaceae

During the Second World War, coconut water was substituted for human blood plasma and administered intravenously in emergency transfusions. The sterile and nutritious properties make it similarly ideal for use in enemas. Although rectal alimentation may sound unsightly, enemas have been popular with everyone from Egyptian Pharaohs to Presidents and Kings throughout history. The oil from a coconut can also be used as a handy lubricant should you want to try it at home. Among all this the most prized and peculiar of all coconut products is the legendary coconut pearl, a naturally occurring gemstone that forms within the fruit. The small white or blueish spheres are exquisite and priceless, famed with mystical properties the emperors of ancient civilizations were said to have had them set in gold and silver to adorn their finest jewellery. Extremely rare, the chances of finding a coconut pearl for your necklace is said to be one in a million; you are statistically more likely to choke on its aquatic namesake while supping an oyster or meet an early grave being killed by a coconut falling from a tree.

Swiss Cheese Plant
Botanical name: *Monstera deliciosa*. Family: Araceae.

Highly poisonous, tiresomely slow to ripen yet etymologically named 'delicious' this fruit is quite a paradox. The flavour resembles something between a pineapple, banana and mango retaining all of the best qualities of each. The all-encompassing taste is so appetising that it has been dubbed the fruit salad plant for its bounty. *Monstera deliciosa* or 'the delicious monster' can kill in a single bite, however, if you dare to take a chance on this reptile-like crop it promises to return ample and unequivocal flavours.

The large fruits are covered in a matrix of hexagonal scales, highly toxic to the touch, taste and smell, and the dragon skin layer emits a pungent gaseous aroma to ward off unwanted predators for miles around.

In order to consume the fleshy pulp within, the fruit must ripen for up to a year until the poisonous external scales are shed revealing the edible insides. Face the monster with bravery and courage for its innards are truly magnificent.

Baobab Fruit

Botanical name: *Adansonia digitata.* Family: Malvaceae

The gargantuan baobab tree can grow upwards of 35m tall and 40m wide, its fruit weighing more than 2kg each. Its mighty core and internal hollows are used for everything from refrigerators to burial chambers, meeting rooms and sleeping quarters.

One particularly large specimen, thought to be the biggest living organism on earth has been turned into a cocktail bar to quench the thirst of locals and flocking tourists alike. 'The Big Baobab' bar is famed for its stiff drinks and cold beers, it features an underground booze cellar and photosynthesising rooftop canopy.

The tree is thought to be the oldest living organism on earth, at around 6,000 years old, and has been around longer than the pyramids in Egypt and Jesus Christ.

When the ancient tree was converted into its present incarnation excavators found tools from Dutch pioneers, and evidence of Bushmen inhabitants. Legend is that the Bushmen believed that the tree had mystical properties and that lions would savage anyone who ate the flowers. Eating the fruit and pips would, however, protect you from crocodiles.

Buddha's Hand Citron

Botanical name: *Citrus medica var. sarcodactylus.* Family: Rutaceae

The Buddha's Hand Citron is a fruit of ancient proverb; it is believed that monks carried the fruit from India to China in the 4th century CE. During the journey an astounding event occurred and the once singular form split into finger-like lobes. Shocked and awed, the monks were convinced of the mystical properties. To add further wonder to the new variety, its uncanny resemblance to a phalange could only be explained as a message from Buddha. The fruity representation of the hands of the deity in prayer has since become a symbol of peace and happiness.

Often since given as a sacred offering, its strong fine fragrance is used to perfume altars and temples. The citrus scent is invigorating and uplifting and inhaling its vapours is said to have an ethereal touch. Equally it can often be found adorning the cash register in Asian grocery stores in the hope of bringing wealth and fortune to the tills.

Pomegranate

Botanical name: *Punica granatum.* Family: Lythraceae

The pomegranate is a fruit with classical gravitas; its fleshy arils are celebrated as both an aphrodisiac and a great symbol of chastity. Ancient Greek legend tells of the Goddess Persephone's only vice; the pomegranate verses the almighty Hades only vice; Persephone and the devastating effects of the ill-matched pair.

The story goes that Hades abducted Persephone to take her to the underworld to be his lover; in protest of her suitor Persephone vowed she would not eat or drink, remaining chaste only except for the few pomegranate seeds that she could not resist. Irritated by this Hades returned to her mother Demeter Goddess of Nature, with the condition that she would be indebted to the underworld for six months of the year, one for every pomegranate seed she had eaten. Demeter mourned the loss of her daughter for these six months preventing any growth in nature and revoking the glory of sunlight as repentance, thus creating the measurable differences between the seasons of winter and summer. Be that a lesson in restraint each time you gorge on the sweet seeds of a pomegranate.

Tomato

Botanical name: *Solanum lycopersicum*. Family: Solanaceae

Closely resembling its botanical relation the deadly nightshade, when the tomato was introduced to Europe in the 16th century the crimson red 'love apple' was immediately associated with sex, sin and the devil. The tomato swiftly gained a reputation for being poisonous; a claim that was in fact substantiated as the high acidity levels reacted with the lead content in popular pewter tableware of the time, resulting in fatal lead poisoning in those who consumed it.

On 26th September 1820 Robert Gibbon Johnson, an American tomato enthusiast, decided to demonstrate once and for all that the tomato was safe to eat. Growing a crop in his back garden, he announced that he would publicly consume the fruit in testimony. Word spread and spectators flocked to watch fully expecting that he would drop dead in front of their very eyes. Johnson of course survived and set up an empire farming tomatoes.

Durian

Botanical name: *Durio zibethinus*. Family: Malvaceae

Often claimed to be the king of fruits the durian is like no other. Regally large the fruit can grow to a colossal 30cm wide and weigh up to 3kg; a healthy durian will dwarf all other fruit in size and allure.

The flavour is dramatically dividing, intense, rich and often slightly fermented, evoking extreme reactions of both hatred and adulation in all who consume it. Be warned, overly excessive durian consumption can result in durian fever, a condition said to be somewhere between the giddy feeling of a first love and that of the flu. When eating the raw flesh of the durian it is recommended that one has a fresh glass of water on hand to counter the curious warming mouth feel.

Banned in many public areas of Singapore and Asia, you can be hit with a substantial fine for taking it on the metro as the fruit expels a potent odour intended to lure in animals from far and wide. Described as resembling the scent of rotting flesh, vomit and faeces it is understandably undesirable in confined spaces. Luckily for its critics durian is a seasonal fruit only available in the summer months. All hail the king of fruits.

The Hunt

By Sam Bompas
Illustration by Emma Rios

The pineapple was long seen as the king of fruits in the UK, a lush and tropical treat combining the bounty of strawberries with an exotic citrus tang. We rate it as a real swashbuckler. It contains the flesh-eating enzyme bromelain, and is useful as a meat tenderiser as well as being the cornerstone of a compelling dessert.

Pineapple fruits were once so rare and wondrous that they would change hands for fortunes. Hostesses would rent them by the hour for dinner parties to impress snobs and rivals.

The 17th-century pineapple mania saw them make the transition from a dinner table delicacy to architectural ornament. This stems from the mariners' practice of attaching a pineapple to the gate on their return home as a symbol of welcome and signifying where a riotous party would be found.

As London natives, we at Bompas & Parr have been obsessed with pineapples in architecture. Gaze across the capital and spot triumphant pineapples as a London-wide architectural motif. The pineapple, a fruit with swagger, is incorporated into masonry, railing and rooftop finials.

With the fruit being a historic symbol of welcome, 2013 is the time to hunt down the city's pineapples. This map, by artist Emma Rios, gives you a head start. It charts some of the notable architectural pineapples. You can find them everywhere from the finials of St Paul's Cathedral to the pineapples of Lambeth Bridge commemorating the first of the fruit to be grown in Britain by John Tradescant the Younger, adventurer, botanist and head gardener to Charles I.

There's also an online version of the map to be found at www.bompasandparr.com. As you discover rare and wonderous architectural fruits add them to the map so it becomes an evolving resource for fruit spotters worldwide. You can also tag photos on Twitter as #tuttifrutti to create a cornucopia of tasty (and ideally tasteful) architecture.

Good hunting. For good measure accompany your pineapple hunts with a Carnival Punch in a hollowed out pineapple (see recipe on page 79).

Hawksmoor Fruit Cup Salad

By Hawksmoor's Queen of Pastry,
Carla Henriques

The challenge? To do fruit salad, Hawksmoor style. Not perhaps the easiest thing when you are a British steakhouse, best known for great hunks of seared meat, chips and cocktails. But perhaps we have something to add … we do, after all, specialise in food that seems simple, but it's deceptively tricky to do incredibly well. So we thought we'd apply our love of British food history and our obsession with adding booze to stuff (from a splash of apple brandy over a Sticky Toffee Pudding to a slug of Jack Daniels in a Crunchie McFlurry).

Here, then, is a recipe you may wish to set aside a little time for, and one that contains that most British of drinks, Pimm's. We recommend you buy more of everything than you need and mix up a jug of Pimm's before you tackle the recipe. Sip leisurely throughout.

James Pimm himself owned a London oyster bar and served his secret concoction to aid digestion in a small tankard known as a 'Number 1 Cup'. Part of a 'booze and fruit' history that goes all the way back to the punches of the 18th Century, Pimm's has, like rain and burnt-yet-raw sausages, become a quintessential ingredient of a British summer.

Fruit Salad
1 cucumber
1 batch spiced sauce (see recipe opposite)
2 lemons
3 oranges
400g fresh strawberries
½ bunch of mint

Wash the cucumber, cut in half and then cut half into long thin slices using a peeling knife or mandolin. The slices should be as thin as possible. Leave the cucumber slices to marinate in the spiced sauce for about 20 minutes, covered. Peel the lemon rind from the lemons and remove the segments. Soak the segments in a small amount of the spiced sauce for about 30 minutes. Peel the oranges and remove any white fibres. Segment the orange and cut the segments in half. Cut the strawberries in half and cut the rest of the cucumber into small cubes. Put the oranges, strawberries and cucumber cubes into a bowl, cover and refrigerate until you are ready to serve.

Crunchy Bites
1½ oranges
35g unsalted butter
30g plain flour
110g caster sugar
5g freshly grated ginger

Grate the oranges carefully taking care not to grate any pith. Squeeze the orange juice and mix with the zest. Soften the butter and mix in with the flour and sugar. Add the orange juice and zest, along with the grated ginger. Cover and refrigerate for 1 hour. Preheat the oven to 180°C/350°F/Gas mark 4. Spread the mixture on a silicone mat or a sheet of baking paper and bake in the oven for 6 minutes until golden brown. Remove from the oven and allow to cool. Break into small pieces and serve.

Pimm's Sorbet
400ml good-quality lemonade
10 mint leaves
180g caster sugar
100ml Pimm's
juice of ½ orange
juice of ½ lemon
2 fresh strawberries, quartered
2cm piece of cucumber, juiced

Heat the lemonade over a low heat for 2 minutes, then add the mint. Bring the lemonade mixture to 40°C, add the sugar and stir until completely dissolved. Add the Pimm's and citrus juices, then pour the mixture into a freezerproof container and freeze for at least 4 hours, stirring occasionally. Strain before serving.

Spiced Sauce
150g caster sugar
200ml water
½ red pepper
2 limes
Cracked black pepper
10 mint leaves, chopped

Dissolve the sugar and water and let it boil for 2 minutes. Slice the red pepper finely and mix it into the syrup, together with the zest of 2 limes and the juice of 1. Add the cracked black pepper and the chopped mint and leave to infuse for about 2 hours.

How to Plate
Mix the marinated lemon segments, orange, strawberry and cucumber cubes together. Serve on cold plates. Tightly roll each slice of the cucumber, cover with 6 tablespoons of spiced sauce and place next to the fruit salad, along with a scoop of Pimm's sorbet on the side. Finish off with a scattering of the crunchy bites.

Hot & Cold Tropical Fruit Salad

By Lily Vanilli. Photography by Nathan Pask

Banana coconut fritters, mixed berry sorbet, chopped frozen blackberries, toasted hazelnuts.

When choosing a fruit to star in my fruit salad I have to go with the blackberry. Probably one of the earliest foods to have been eaten by humans, they've been a part of our diet for thousands of years.

There's charm in the way this invasive weed with pitch black fruit roams free, growing wild in ditches and by roadsides. The poetry of the blackberry bush has not been lost on others and it has often entered folklore and myth. Christ's blood was said to have manifested itself in blackberries, and his crown of thorns was a bramble.

They're supposedly loathed by the Devil and a bad omen, just touching them was said to bring you bad luck. In Greek myth when Bellerophon fell from Pegasus trying to seize the Gods' powers he fell into a blackberry bush, was maimed and blinded and lived the rest of his life as an outcast.

This all seems a bit unfair, as their medicinal properties have been recognised for centuries, and their berries and leaves provide free catering. Like most fruits they work wonderfully in almost anything baked but are always at their best when fresh. This fruit salad dessert is hot and cold and the berries should melt on your tongue releasing a burst of flavour.

serves 4

Ingredients
Banana Coconut **Fritters**
(recipe opposite – make fresh before serving)
Mixed Berry Sorbet
(recipe opposite – make at least a day ahead)
A handful of ripe blackberries, frozen
A handful of toasted hazelnuts, roughly chopped

Banana Coconut **Fritters**
60g plain flour
½ tsp bicarbonate of soda
1 egg
4½ tbsp desiccated coconut
1 tbsp golden caster sugar
1 tbsp light brown sugar
pinch of good vanilla
pinch of sea salt
60ml water
4 ripe bananas
1 cup vegetable oil, for frying

In a large bowl, sift the flour and bicarbonate of soda and combine evenly, then add all the rest of the ingredients except the bananas and oil. Whisk to a smooth batter. Heat the oil for frying in a heavy-based pan to 190°C.

Meanwhile, peel the bananas and slice each in half, then half lengthways.

Dip the bananas in the batter until coated, then shake off any excess batter and carefully lower them into the hot oil. Flip as soon as the batter turns golden brown and fry evenly on the other side. Remove and drain on kitchen paper. Be ready to serve these quick and hot.

Mixed Berry Sorbet
3 cups fresh or frozen mixed berries of your choice, blackberries, raspberries, blueberries, red or blackcurrants all work well
210g caster sugar
2 cups water
finely grated zest and juice of a lime

Place all the ingredients in a medium saucepan over a medium-high heat and bring to the boil. Once boiling, reduce the heat to low and simmer for 10 minutes to thicken.

Remove from the heat and pulse the mixture with a hand-held blender, you may wish to also pass the mixture through a fine sieve.

Transfer in an ice-cream machine and churn following the manufacturer's instructions. After it is churned, transfer the sorbet to the freezer to set overnight.

To Serve
Rough chop the frozen blackberries. Put the hot fritters on a plate with a scoop of sorbet (not touching). Sprinkle with the chopped hazelnuts and finally the frozen blackberries. Serve immediately.

Rubix Fruit Salad

By Joe Wagenaar, Head Pastry Chef,
Andaz Liverpool Street

Here's a dish first created for the Dinner of Epochs, a gustatory adventure to mark the 5th Anniversary of the Andaz Hotel.

The meal was so vast, so grand and so magnificent it spanned hundreds of years of history and three of the restaurants across the hotel. Guests changed dining room with each successive course for a meal that featured a candlelit Masonic temple, Pollia condensata berries, reckless toasting, and culminated with the final course served on a table with entirely liquid surface.

Hot & Cold Tropical Fruit Salad: Loathed by the devil but will melt on your tongue

This Rubix Fruit Salad was the centerpiece of that final course raised above the neon fluid surface of the table on slate pedestals. Some skill was required in eating it – the liquid tabletop meant that it was impossible to rest elbows on the table with further hazard coming from the leeches loose beneath the surface. The liquid did have the advantage of stabilising the final wine, a 2002 Tokaji Aszú 5 Puttonyos, at 13°C – ideal for balancing freshness, flavour release and connoisseurship.

Serves 2

One 6cm Cube
¼ watermelon
½ cantaloupe melon
½ gala melon
3 kiwi fruits
10 strawberries
2 mangos
1 dragon fruit

Preparation
Wash and peel all the fruits. Each Cube requires 27 small cubes with dimensions of 2cm each. Use 4 pieces of each fruit per Cube (you will only be able to use 3 pieces of 1 fruit).

Cut the fruit at straight angles using a ruler to measure out 2cm cubes. Once you have perfect cubes, use them as a template to cut the remaining pieces.

Pipette syrups

Spiced Passion Fruit and Lemongrass
1 piece lemongrass
1 cinnamon stick
3 cloves
375ml water
180g granulated sugar
100g passion fruit purée
zest of ½ orange
zest of ½ lemon
1 passion fruit

Bruise the lemongrass and spices with a rolling pin.

Put all the ingredients in a pan except the passion fruit and bring slowly to the boil.

Simmer for 5 minutes, then remove from the heat, and add the pulp of the passion fruit.

Leave the mixture to infuse overnight. Strain out the spices and seeds and serve.

Sour Cherry Syrup
75g granulated sugar
200g sour cherry purée
10ml lemon juice
50ml cherry Kirsch

Boil the sugar, purée and lemon juice. Remove from the heat, add the Kirsch and serve.

Minted Absinthe Syrup
75g granulated sugar
100ml water
100g fresh mint leaves
100ml absinthe

Boil the sugar and water in a pan. Allow to cool to 25°C, then add the mint leaves, cover and leave overnight in the fridge.

Blitz the sugar syrup with the mint and pass through a sieve. Reserve the mint pulp left over.

Put 30g of the mint pulp back into the syrup along with the absinthe.

To Serve
Form the rubix cube ensuring no fruit square is placed beside its brother fruit. Fill the pipettes with the assorted syrups and serve alongside.

Flaming Fruit Inferno

By Abi Shapiro of Bompas & Parr

Flambéed dishes make for a pumping and provocative grand finalé for your meal, the combination of heat, light and potential danger adding a rush of adrenaline to the dining experience. The best time to introduce flambé to your dinner table is during the dessert course, as this is when your guests will be most in need of a fiery inferno to arouse them from their postprandial slump.

Three of the best known, and most commonly reproduced flambé dishes were all allegedly created for special occasions, unsurprising, as few dishes impress as much as an edible fireball. Crêpes Suzette was first (accidentally!) made for the future King Edward VII in 1895; Cherries Jubilee was designed by Auguste Escoffier especially for Queen Victoria's Diamond Jubilee in 1897, and Bananas Foster was created for Richard Foster, the New Orleans Crime Commission chairman, in 1951.

Setting fire to the fruit not only provides an impressive spectacle, but also changes the taste of the dish. Adding alcohol adds flavour and aroma to a dish; setting light to the dish then reduces the raw alcoholic tones, and leaves the rich, deep flavours of the spirit. As the sugar heats, it will begin to caramelise, which again adds another delicious dimension to the dessert.

The result is an orgy of fruit for your tongue, coated in the taboo of hot, buttery, alcoholic sauce.

The Flaming Fruit Inferno combines the sensual flavours of the three classic flambé desserts above, and uses ingredients that visually match the eponymous flames of the dish. The reds, oranges and yellows of the fruit combine to make a beautiful dish even after the flames have gone out.

Brave, experienced or foolish flambéers can add an extra element of showmanship by adding the following items to the fruit once it's alight:

Ground cinnamon will produce sparks when added to the flames.

A pinch of salt will produce yellow flames.

Most salt substitutes (that contain potassium chloride) will produce a purple flame.

Using Calvados instead of brandy will give much taller flames.

Please take all precautions when making this dish, and make sure that you have a lid readily available to place on top of the pan if necessary.

Serves 8

Ingredients
3 bananas
2 oranges
600g cherries, stalks removed and stoned
100g butter
200g light brown sugar
50ml Calvados
50ml dark rum
50ml Cointreau
8 scoops vanilla ice cream, to serve

Peel the bananas and oranges and cut into bite-sized pieces. Ensure that the cherries have all their stalks and stones removed. Melt the butter in a large frying pan over a medium heat and add the sugar, stirring until dissolved. Add the cherries and stir gently, for about 4 minutes, until they begin to soften.

Add the bananas and oranges to the pan and cook for further 4 minutes, turning occasionally, and spooning the sauces over the fruit. Allow to soften until slightly browned.

Combine the Calvados, rum and Cointreau in a glass, reduce the heat and add the mixture to the pan. Allow the alcohol to heat gently, then light the contents of the pan with a long match, standing well back until the flames subside. Once the flames have gone out, stir and serve over ice cream.

Beats in Tangiers

By Yinka Shonibare MBE

The beatnik generation included primary figures William S. Burroughs, Jack Kerouac and Allen Ginsburg. Among their drug-induced writer travels, Tangiers, Morocco famously appears in their lives, a feature of both literary and personal wanderings.

This dish is inspired by those famous 'interzone' days and may perhaps transport you back to the notorious Beat hangout Café de Paris in Place de France, Tangiers.

Serves 4–6

Ingredients
1 mandarin, peeled and cut into bite-sized pieces
2 bananas, peeled and cut into bite-sized pieces
5–6 strawberries, cut in half
2–3 Medjool dates, cut into bite-sized pieces
10 fresh mint leaves, torn, plus extra whole leaves to decorate
2–3 fresh figs, quartered
(or Turkish figs, cut into bite-sized pieces)
2 tbsp orange flower water
3–4 tbsp honey (adjust for ripeness of fruit)
1–2 tsp ground cinnamon
¼ cup toasted almonds, to decorate

Place all the prepared fruits and mint leaves in a bowl, except for the fresh figs (if dried figs are being used then add to the mix) and almonds.

In a separate dish, add the orange blossom water and honey and mix until the honey is blended well with the water.

Pour the honey orange flower blossom water mixture over the prepared fruit, add the cinnamon and toss together to make sure all the fruit is coated. Add the fresh figs at the end as they tend to be much more delicate. Leave the fruit to stand for 1–2 hours, or preferably overnight before serving.

Put a small frying pan on a medium-high heat, add the almonds (which can be chopped if preferred) and toast for 2–4 minutes, stirring regularly to not to overroast. Remove the pan from the heat and leave to cool.

Serve the fruit with its 'juice', topped with pieces of almond and fresh mint to decorate.

Helpful Hints
You can use any fruit you like. Citrus fruit works well as it adds a nice 'sauce' to the dessert, it also softens the dates and figs and brings out their sugars into the mix.

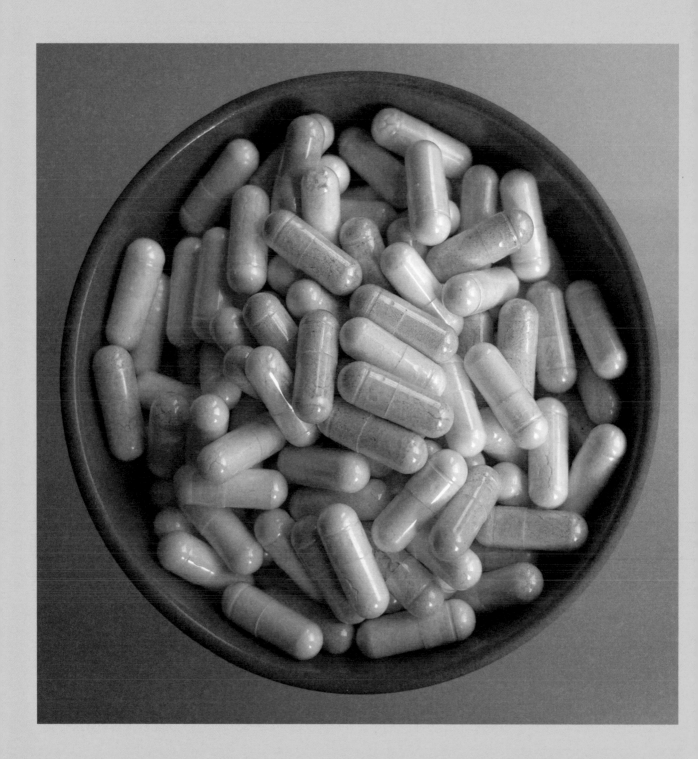

The forbidden fruit of the pill party

Fruit Salad Pill Party

By Caitlin Williams Freeman

According to the Internet, in the 1960's and 70's, a party craze known as 'fruit salad parties' was reported to be all the rage. Kids would raid their parents' medicine cabinets, bringing to a party miscellaneous pills that would be combined, fruit salad-like, into a bowl for blind consumption. I like to imagine that, had I been alive back then, I would have been the square who got the plan all wrong, invited my friends over for fruit, and disappointed everyone when they discovered that there were no drugs involved in my party. Which is exactly what I'm proposing you do here.

I use freeze-dried fruit when making these pill-encased sherbets, which you can find in the market under the label Just Fruit.

Ingredients
½ cup/10g freeze-dried fruit (such as banana, raspberry, blueberry, mango, pineapple or apple)
⅓ cup/38g icing sugar
1 tbsp/10g citric acid
1 tsp bicarbonate of soda
50 extra large size gel capsules
(size 000, 1.37ml volume)

In a spice grinder or whirly blade coffee grinder, pulse the freeze-dried fruit until it is a powder.

Add the icing sugar, citric acid and bicarbonate of soda, and whizz until it is a fine powder with a unified colour. Pour into a small bowl.

Separate the gel capsule and fill each end with powder. Over the bowl, fit the gel capsule back together, and then wipe the edges with a clean, dry, cloth.

Combine capsules of different flavours in a bowl. Store any leftovers in an airtight container.

The Albino Peacock White Fruit Salad

By Abi Shapiro of Bompas & Parr

Nearly all fruits are a real treat to the eye, with some of nature's most striking colours making the fruit's appearance as enjoyable as its taste. The bright tones are an important part of the plants' reproduction and survival techniques, serving to attract animals to help to spread the seeds of the fruit. The pigment that provides the colour in the fruit also protects the plant from being harmed by UV rays and allows the plant to photosynthesise. The bright colours are caused by various pigments; bright greens come from the presence of chlorophyll, purple and red fruits contain anthocyanins, and orange and red fruits contain carotenoids.

Many of these fruits limit their bold visual features to the exterior of their form, and once the bright outer skin has been removed, a much paler flesh is revealed. Feasting on a salad of white-fleshed fruit allows you to focus fully on the flavour and textural components of the fruit. With no colour cues to aid recognition of the ingredients, you must rely on your taste buds alone to identify the exotic blend of sweet and juicy elements. The ingredients have been carefully chosen to provide an explosive taste sensation, and the variety of textures will provide sharp crunch, soft chew, and smooth gulp in the same mouthful.

Serves 8

Ingredients
2 apples
3 bananas
½ coconut
4 mangosteens
2 dragon fruit
12 rambutans
½ honeydew melon
2 custard apples
12 lychees
500ml plain yogurt, to taste (optional)
bright peels of your choice, to decorate

Peel All the Fruit
The simplest way to peel the mangosteen is to cut around the diameter with a sharp knife, ensuring the fruit inside is not punctured. The two sides will then pull apart, and the flesh can be removed.

To peel the dragon fruit, pull downwards on one of the leaves and peel with a similar technique to a banana.

To peel the rambutan, make a small incision with a knife, and use your fingers to squeeze the fruit out.

Remove the seeds from the melon, mangosteens, custard apples, lychees and rambutans, then cut all the fruit into bite-sized pieces and put in a serving bowl. Gently mix all the ingredients. Add yogurt to taste and stir. Decorate with a selection of bright peels of your choice.

Further Uses of the Peel
While the inner flesh is the true hero of the fruit, and is generally perceived to be the sole purpose of the plant, the beautiful protective natural packaging of the fruit should not be forgotten. Providing bright, garish

temptation, the distinct shape and colour of the fruit draws you in from across the room, and the fruit display is the visual highlight of any retail outlet, providing the ultimate marketing tool. The skin does not have to be discarded after it has been removed, and often has even more effective health benefits than the flesh itself. Here are some of the ways in which fruit skin can make your life healthier and happier:

Apples

The ursolic acid in apple peel has been found to reduce cholesterol and blood sugar, to help build muscle and reduce body fat. It has also been suggested that it can have a positive impact on obesity and diabetes, and reduce the likelihood of strokes and heart attacks.

Bananas

Rubbing the inside of a banana skin directly on to your body can have amazing results, and has been known to soothe itchy insect bites and rashes, increase the rate at which bruises heal, remove warts, aid healing of scratches, heal psoriasis and reduce outbreaks of acne. When applied to the forehead, the skin helps cure headaches and tightens the skin, reducing wrinkles. Other uses for banana skins include removing splinters, and teeth whitening by rubbing the skin on your teeth every day.

Coconut

Grinding down the hard shell of the coconut and adding to a standard moisturiser will create an effective exfoliator. The smell from the smoke produced by burning the shell of a coconut will also repel mosquitos.

Custard Apple

Drinking tea brewed from the skin of a custard apple will cure pneumonia, although should be ingested in small quantities as it can cause temporary paralysis. If dried, ground into a powder and applied to the head, the custard apple skin can kill lice.

Dragon Fruit

The skin of the dragon fruit is extremely high in flavonoids, which have antibacterial, antioxidant, anti-inflammatory and antiviral effects. They also reduce the risk of cardiovascular problems, and could limit the growth of cancerous cells.

Lychee

Drinking a tea made from the peel of lychees boosts the immune system, and can treat diarrhoea and smallpox, as well as common infections including coughs and colds.

Mangosteen

Slice the skin into pieces and remove the very dark outer layer of peel. Clean the skin and blend it to create a juice that is extremely high in antioxidants. The skin of a mangosteen cures skin diseases, heart disease, thrombosis and hypertension. It is claimed that the peel can also treat various cancers as well as asthma, Alzheimer's, acne, bronchitis, diarrhoea, pneumonia, Parkinson's disease, ulcers, and even limits the progress to other cells of the HIV virus. Mangosteen skin is also believed to be an antidepressant, aids weight loss, and repairs damaged skin cells to keep your skin looking youthful.

Melon

Boiling the skin of a melon and rubbing the resulting concoction directly onto the head is said to encourage new hair growth, and eradicates dandruff and dry skin.

Rambutan

Dry the skin of the rambutan, and then wash thoroughly. Add several cups of water and bring to the boil. Drinking this liquid will reduce fever, cure dysentery and treat diarrhoea. It also treats oral thrush and will make your hair darker.

Fruit Salad Cirino

By Michael Cirino of a razor, a shiny knife
Photography by Noah Kalina

Over the past decade I have been looking at cooking as a process to be enjoyed instead of as a means to an end – the idea that the act of creation is equal to, if not greater than, the act of consumption. Moving from work that is required to create a meal that will be enjoyed with friends into a celebration where the pleasure is derived from the process, this social interaction creates an open forum for friends to teach, interact and learn from each other. This simple fruit salad recipe represents a creative inspiration born in a friendly kitchen with a group of friends discussing what would be possible if... ...we had liquid nitrogen... ...we could throw a dinner party with our friends in the heart of London in a Victorian citadel that was steeped with the darkness embedded in its walls from the misguided passions of the era in which it was built... ...we wanted to try something difficult...

In the end, this salad is an amalgamation of ideas that alone would be lost and wayward, stuck in the ether between our imaginations and the world we interact with. Trapped as an idea lost to the winds of casual conversation had a group of friends not come together and insisted that it must exist, that its existence was

Fruit Salad Cirino: blackberry and the act of creation

of great enough value to give it a purpose, a purpose strong enough to make it become real.

This dish juxtaposes sweet and savoury, elegant and modest, while exciting the palate with a unique combination of creamy dairy, briny ocean, and tart fruit. I hope you enjoy.

Blackberry, Caviar, Cream Cheese
Black Brioche
337.20g plain flour
6.00g fast action dried yeast
108.00g whole milk
2.40 eggs, lightly beaten
204.00g butter, softened
30.00g white sugar
24.00g sepia, (squid ink)
12.00g salt

Put the flour and yeast in the bowl of a freestanding mixer fitted with a paddle. Add the milk and eggs and beat at medium speed until you have a smooth dough. Pulse the butter a few pieces at a time and beat at medium speed until completely incorporated. Change the paddle to a dough hook, add the sugar and salt and mix on low speed until combined. Increase the speed to medium-high and knead the dough until glossy and very elastic, about 12–15 minutes.

Spray a bowl with cooking spray, scrape the dough into the bowl, then turn the dough over. Cover tightly with cling film and refrigerate overnight.

Spray a 23 x 13cm loaf tin with cooking spray. Flatten the dough into a 20 x 30cm rectangle and roll the dough tightly, starting with the short side and pressing down firmly as you roll. As you reach the far end flatten with the heel of your hand, then finish rolling. Place the dough seam side down in the loaf tin, then cover with clingfilm and leave to rise until doubled in size, about 2 hours.

Preheat the oven to 180°C/350°F/Gas mark 4. Uncover the brioche and bake for 30 minutes. Reduce the oven temperature to 160°C/325°F/Gas mark 3 and bake for another 30–45 minutes until the crust is crisp and the loaf sounds hollow when tapped on the base. Remove from the tin and leave to cool on a wire rack.

Blackberry Sauce
120.00g blackberries
120.00g white sugar
120.00ml water
0.10% 0.36g xanthan gum

Place the fruit, sugar and water in a pan and bring to the boil over a high heat. Do not macerate the berries. Reduce until sweet, then strain and process in a blender at low speed while adding the xanthan gum into the vortex. Chill in the fridge until needed.

Fluffy Cream Cheese
100.00g cream cheese
20.00g double cream

Place the cream cheese and cream in a freestanding mixer and whip until fluffy, then place in a large piping bag. Prepare right before service. Keep refrigerated.

Blackberry Caviar
80.00g blackberries
16.00g blackberry sauce

Freeze the blackberries in LN_2, then shatter and separate the seeds from the pith.

Place the blackberries drooplets into a bowl and freeze for 20 minutes.

Mix a small amount of the chilled blackberry sauce with the frozen drooplets to form a thick mixture. Prepare at least 1 hour before service. Keep refrigerated.

For service
6.00 Black Brioche Loaves
120.00g Fluffy Cream Cheese
40.00g Blackberry Caviar
8.00g black finishing salt
60.00 chives

Slice the brioche and toast lightly, then cut into triangles. Pipe the Fluffy Cream cheese on to the pointed end of each toast. Strain the blackberry arils and chill the sauce.

Mix the blackberry caviar and blackberry arils in a small bowl and coat sparingly with the blackberry syrup and salt to taste. Top the cream cheese with the caviar and 2 pieces of chive.

La Pêche Adele

By Alexis Gauthier of Gauthier Soho

The peach has seduced us French for centuries.

Legend has it, Louis XIV was massively obsessed with the fruit and wanted to eat them all. He famously named varieties after his mistresses, dogs, servants and had an entire orchard planted in Versailles. 'Roi Soleil', as Louis XIV was known, was probably convinced that his own enlightenment would ripen the fruits.

Then in 1892 London, French chef Auguste Escoffier created a dessert for the famous Australian opera singer Nellie Melba, combining sweet soaked peaches with vanilla ice cream. It would sound slightly pejorative, ironic or super-naff now to create such a basic dessert, but back then it was the high of refinement. How on earth had anybody not thought of sandwiching a spoon of vanilla ice cream in between two lobes of peach prior Escoffier is quite unbelievable.

So I want to bring it into the 21st century and celebrate this classic but slightly trashy pairing of syrupy sweetness and creaminess. I also want to use modern food packaging and technology to inform the flavour and texture of the dish.

The magic is the maceration of the tinned peach in its own syrup so it is always at that perfect point of softness, without falling apart. It has lost any unpleasant toughness you sometimes get with fresh peach flesh. The industrialised vanilla ice cream is also important in its richness and the way it sticks together even when not frozen – purely using magical postwar added jellying agents.

As the real Nellie Melba might be slightly retired from duties these days I've decided to dedicate it to her present day equivalent and product of modern Grande-Bretagne: Adele.

Adele is the perfect partner to the peach – La Peche Adele: Popular, fun, slightly mainstream, pure product of the commercial world but fantastic at her job.

Escoffier justified his creation on the fact that Melba had some fragile vocal cords; just like Adele! Different era, same remedies.

Serves 4

Ingredients
400g fresh raspberries
40g icing sugar
juice of ½ lemon
125g drained tinned lychees in syrup
2 tins of peaches in syrup (8 halves peaches)
200g caster sugar
100ml water

4 tsp sunflower oil
½ litre tub of Classic Vanilla Häagen-Dazs® ice cream
1 tub of Cool Whip whipping cream

Reserve half of the raspberries for the decoration. Put the other half in a blender with the icing sugar and lemon juice and blitz until puréed. Cut the lychees into small cubes (5 x 5mm), then place them in a bowl and add 2 spoons of the raspberry coulis. Keep the coulis and reserved raspberries in the fridge until plating.

Drain the peaches making sure not to press too much on them, as they need to retain a certain amount of their liquid. Place them face down on a plate and keep them in the fridge covered with cling film.

Put a heavy-based pan on the hob and add the caster sugar and water. Let the water and sugar boil until it starts turning brown. Do not stir with a spoon at any moment as it will blur the caramel.

Oil a large baking tray with the vegetable oil then pour the caramel over it. Gently move the tray making sure that the caramel is uniformly spread over the tray. Wait 2 minutes until the caramel starts cooling down then flap it over on a clean surface. Break the caramel in small pieces with a large knife.

Plating La Pêche Adele
Line 4 large soup plates and pour 3 spoons of raspberry coulis in each one of them. Place half a peach in the middle of each plate and top it with some small scoops of vanilla ice cream (use a warm spoon to scoop the vanilla ice cream out of the tub).

Top the ice cream with some lychees and cover them with some small amounts of whipping cream. Place some fresh raspberries in the cream and cover them with another half peach. Take a lot of small pieces of caramel and plant them into the peach. Pour the remaining coulis over and serve at once.

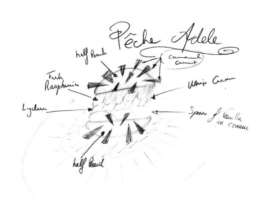

Here's how Alexis sees it

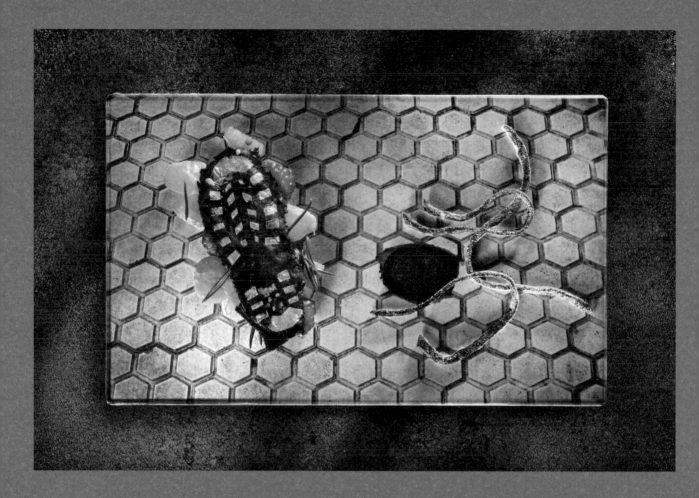

Fruta Pisada by José López

Fruta Pisada

By Elena Arzak of Arzak. Photograpy by José López

Ingredientes (Para 4 Per.):

Para los cordones
60g de jarabe base
10g de glucosa
30g de cacao en polvo
Pizca de polvo de plata

Para el cuajado de mole y albaricoque
390g de puré de albaricoque
60g de mole negro
4 huevos
100g de azúcar
20g de brandy
75g de azúcar (caramelo)

Para el azúcar especiado
60g de azúcar
1g de tomillo seco
1g de regaliz en polvo
1g de jengibre en polvo
1g de pimienta negra en polvo
1g de perejil seco en polvo

Para las frutas
½ mango
1 naranja
50g de coco fresco pelado
½ manzana
60 de piña pelada
4 fresas
1 melocotón
(*) Podríamos utilizar cualquier fruta de temporada

Para la base negra y su pisada
1 clara de huevo
150g de azúcar glass
150g de almendra molida
2g de tinta de chipirón
Plantilla con forma de pisada
Pizca de oro en polvo

Elaboracion

Para los cordones
Mezclar el conjunto de los ingredientes excepto la plata y dejar reposar durante 24 horas en frío. Introducir el conjunto en una manga y estirar sobre una silpat del tamaño de unos cordones de zapato. Hornear durante 2 minutos a 200ºC. Retirar y espolvorearlos con plata en polvo.

Para el cuajado de mole y albaricoque
Caramelizar los 75g de azúcar y verterlos sobre unos moldes rectangulares de flexipan.
Triturar bien en la thermomix el resto de los ingredientes y verter el conjunto sobre el molde.
Cocer durante 70 minutos a 100ºC.

Para el azúcar especiado
Mezclar todos los ingredientes. Reservar.

Para las frutas
Limpiar y pelar las frutas. Cortarlas en trozos no muy grandes. Espolvorear de azúcar especiado las frutas y saltearlas levemente sobre un colador a la brasa de carbón vegetal hasta que se doren.

Para la base negra y su pisada
Amasar la almendra junto con el azúcar, la clara y la tinta. Estirar la masa dando formas irregulares.
Con la ayuda de una lámina de plástico de pastelería realizaremos unos cortes dándole forma de una pisada.
Posaremos la plantilla sobre la base negra y pintaremos con el oro, retirando la plantilla y descubriendo la pisada.
Hornear durante 8 minutos a 160ºC.

Finaly Presentacion
Sobre un recipiente, que represente la acera de una calle, colocar en primer lugar el cuajado y sobre ellos las frutas. Tapando todo ello dispondremos la pisada. Terminar colocando los cordones al lado de la pisada.

Fruit Salad Ambrosias

By Olivia Bennett of Bompas & Parr

Our fruit salad ambrosias offer a range of flavours and viscosities from a simplest syrup to thick lavender creams. They give you a choice to complement the rainbow spectrum of sweet fruit flesh available to your experienced palate.

Use them on whatever tasty combo of fruit you have to hand.

Classic Ambrosia

This is a spiced vanilla syrup to complement the simple pleasure of ripe fruit.

Ingredients
2 vanilla pods
5 cardamom pods
1 star anise
200g granulated sugar
3 tbsp honey
200ml water
25ml lemon juice

Halve the vanilla pods and scoop out the seeds then place them with the cardamom, star anise, sugar, honey and water in a pan. Bring to the boil, stirring until all the sugar has dissolved, then sieve to remove the spices and allow to cool.

Serving suggestion
Serve on a sunny combination of sliced peaches and mangoes. For a great breakfast add extra syrup and pile the fruit into a crêpe pancake.

Yellow Fever Ambrosia

3cm piece of fresh ginger
2 red bird's eye chillies
juice of 2 limes
juice of 1 lemon
100ml soy sauce
100g palm sugar
200ml jasmine tea, strongly brewed

Make the ambrosia by finely chopping the ginger and chillies then combining with the citrus juices, soy sauce, palm sugar and jasmine tea.

Serving suggestion
Here's a suggestion adapted from the traditional Tom Sum:

Fruits
2 papayas, finely grated
1/4 watermelon, peeled and finely sliced
Bunch of Thai basil, roughly chopped

Finely grate the papaya into noodle-like strands. Place in a serving bowl and add the watermelon (which is not traditionally included but makes for a more thirst-quenching dessert). Gently toss the ingredients together, then add some roughly chopped Thai basil.
Alternatively, you can make this into a tasty meal by adding pan-fried cashew nuts, coriander, mixed salad leaves and about 60g chopped feta.

Lime Slime

Photography by Nathan Pask

This recipe is inspired by the 55,000 litre Rose's Lime cordial jelly we made to surround the SS Great Britain, Brunel's ironclad ship moored in Bristol. Rose's cordial was a favourite for sailors, and closest they came to scurvy cure. The alginate thickens the syrup for a super intense sweet tangy side for fruits.

Ingredients
50ml lime juice (strained for pulp and seeds)
20ml lemon juice (strained for pulp and seeds)
120ml sugar syrup (see page 55)
100ml fresh lemonade/or seltzer
3/4 tsp sodium alginate
Green food dye to a pleasing colour

Combine all the ingredients in a food processor. Slowly add the sodium alginate while pulsing the processor so it thickens without forming any unsightly lumps of powder.
While you are doing this, marinate on the logistical challenges faced when making a similar recipe to set the SS Great Britain in the fruity gel matrix, two Olympic swimming pools in length.

Serving suggestion
Engulf any fruits you like in this slimy and memorable sauce. A word of warning: use sparingly.

Lime Slime: The taboo of a thickened sauce will linger on. Use Sparingly

Fruit Bubbles: Use a slotted spoon to serve over fruit

Fruit Bubbles

Photography by Nathan Pask

Here's a recipe given to us by Australian pastry chefs Burch & Purchese. The recipe is hard work but pretty special spooned over fruit.

Ingredients
750ml mineral water
250ml cherry juice
10g acai berry powder
2g xanthan gum mesh 200
20g caster sugar
1g salt
20g egg white powder

Combine 650ml of the water with the cherry juice and mix the berry powder in slowly. All the water must be incorporated and there must be no trace of bubbles, lumps or foam. Strain this mixture through a fine chinois. Incorporate the xanthan, sugar and salt. Place the mixture in a bowl and mix super slowly so as not to form bubbles or foam or break the xanthan.

In a mortar, place the egg white powder and add the remaining water (100ml) in a slow thin stream, working the mixture with a spoon to make a thin paste. Move the powder slowly and eradicate any lumps by pressing with the spoon against the side of the mortar. Leave to stand for 15 minutes to settle. Squeeze out any air and add this to the mixture to your main mixing bowl. Mix slowly for 25 minutes and place the mixture in the fridge at 5C. Allow to rest for a day.

Using an aquarium pump, push air into the mix forming 'bubbles'. Alternatively, use a straw to gently create bubbles across the surface.

Serving suggestion
Scoop up the bubbles with a spoon and serve them with red cherries, and a scoop of crushed ice laced with vanilla syrup.

Jamaican Ambrosia

Ingredients
110g light brown sugar
2 cinnamon sticks
275ml water
finely grated zest and juice of 2 limes
100ml fresh orange juice
100ml pineapple juice
2 passion fruit

2 tbsp dark rum
grated nutmeg

Put the sugar, cinnamon and water in a small saucepan, then add the lime zest. Heat slowly over a gentle heat until all the sugar has dissolved, about 5 minutes.

Stir with a wooden spoon – you should have no sugar crystals left clinging to the spoon when you turn it over. Remove the pan from the heat, sieve and allow to cool.

Add all the juices, passion fruit and rum and chill until ready for use. Grate on the nutmeg just before using so it's fresh!

Serving suggestion
1 pineapple
1 guava, cut into cubes
20 strawberries, hulled and sliced
30 blueberries
10 lychees
2 kiwi fruits, peeled and cubed
2 orange peeled and cubed
1 banana, finely sliced
grated nutmeg

Chop all the fruits into a bowl and slosh in your chilled Jamaican ambrosia. As you serve the fruit salad, sprinkle a little freshly grated nutmeg over each serving. Tropical!

Spiked Gin Cream

This thick and moreish ambrosia and is so calorific it is equally delicious served in winter or summer.

Ingredients
600ml double cream
120ml sugar syrup (see page 55)
2 lavender sprigs
120ml Tanqueray Gin

Lightly whip the double cream until just before it begins to form soft peaks.

Infuse the sugar syrup with the lavender in a pan and bring to the boil. Reduce the heat and simmer for 10 minutes. Sieve the syrup to remove any floaters and add a heavy slug of gin. Slowly fold into the cream.

Serving suggestion
Serve with fresh berries such as blackberries, raspberries, blueberries or whatever you like. Straight to the point in a homage to the Scottish highlands.

Genetically modified bacteria synthesise the same enzymes that make jellyfish and fireflies glow in the dark

Bioluminescent Durian Sauce

By Sam Bompas. Photography by Beth Evans

For the first time in the history of mankind, you can make a fruit salad ambrosia that fluoresces with the same enzymes that make jellyfish bioluminescent. When you see fireflies light up they are combining the naturally occurring chemicals, luciferase and CTZ that with some resourceful internet shopping you can add to your to your fruit salad sauce to make it glow in the dark.

The trouble is that the enzymes are both pH sensitive and don't taste very good. The trick is to put on a good show by first demonstrating the effect with a clear sugar syrup. Then finish the sauce with puréed durian, the odoriferous and haunting fruit the consumption of which is said to be 'like eating your favourite ice cream while sat on the loo'. While its flesh tastes sweet like caramel or banana pudding, the penetrating odour has been compared to cat sick, sewage, old socks and body odour. As durian is the fruit equivalent of an acid trip, it is totally appropriate for the unusual sauce you about to make.

Ingredients
200ml sugar syrup
The flesh of half a durian (makes a great purée)
1g powdered luciferin
5ml Pure alcohol (overproof rum will also do)
0.1g CTZ

Make a batch of sugar syrup by bringing 100ml water to the boil, tipping in 100g sugar, then removing from the heat and stirring until dissolved. Leave to cool.

Purée the durian flesh so that there's enough for all of your guests to have alongside their fruit salad. Don't worry you are not alone. The smell is enough to make anyone into a mouth breather.

When the syrup has cooled, slowly mix the powdered luciferin into the liquid using a whisk or fork to beat it in, ensuring it doesn't clump. Store in a beautiful clear glass vessel for service. This is where the spectacular glowing reaction will happen.

Suck the alcohol into a pipette and mix with the CTZ ensuring it is fully dissolved. Then suck the combined mixture back into the pipette.

When you have the pipette with CTZ dissolved in alcohol, the glass flask with luciferin in sugar syrup, and an elegant bowl of the durian purée you are ready for service. Let the show commence.

A certain degree of showmanship is needed. The less light there is, the better this will work. If you can do it in total darkness, so much the better. We like to do this trick in the pitch black.

With a flourish add a single drop from the pipette into the glass flask. A beautiful fluorescence will blossom and your guests will gasp. Then hit them with a full squirt of the entire contents of the pipette. The all-natural glow is enchanting.

It's up to you to read the table. Make sure you end on a high. Before you lose their attention (and the effect finishes) mix the fluorescing syrup into the durian purée. The acidity will kill the glow but the powerful flavour will disguise how repellent bioluminescent enzymes can taste!

Medley of Iced Fruits

By Olivia Bennett of Bompas & Parr

An elegant way of presenting frozen fruit granitas or ice creams is to hull out the fruit, use the juices to create a flavoursome ice and refreeze back in the original fruity casing. The principle can be applied to a greater or lesser extent to pretty much any fruit you care to think of – soft skinned fruits will require a lot more artistry to master than their harder skinned fellows.

Visually punchy, the trick is used to fancy up desserts in entry level Asian and Italian joints. It's a simple procedure, but applying the principal to a whole medley of fruits you can create a cornucopia of frozen pleasure. Here we provide three recipes by way of example. Use your imagination and the same principle to give guests ocular and alvine satisfaction.

Pomegranate & Rose Sorbet in Pomegranate
To fill 2 pomegranates
200ml pomegranate juice (from the pomegranates)
25ml lemon juice
150ml sugar syrup (see page 55)
100ml blood orange juice
12ml rose extract
50ml water

This recipe is a take on Persian flavours and is both refreshing and visually opulent to serve alone or with other varieties of ices to create a medley.

Cut the pomegranate in half vertically and scoop out jewel-like red arils. Reserve the hollowed pomegranate halves and a few arils. You are going to use the rest of the pomegranate arils from the fruit to flavour the ice. Start by carefully removing the pips from the arils. Blend the arils in a food processor to yield the juice before sieving it.

Combine with the lemon juice, sugar syrup, blood orange juice, rose extract and water. Pour into a pre-frozen ice-cream machine and churn for 10 minutes to soft sorbet consistency. Then pile back into the reserved pomegranate halves and place in the freeze to fully freeze. Alternatively, freeze the mixture in a shallow tray, stirring every half an hour with a fork until frozen to sorbet consistency. To serve scatter the halves with fresh pomegranate arils.

Dragon Fruit ice cream in Dragon fruit
To fill 2 dragon fruits
300g dragon fruit
100ml coconut water
25ml lime juice
200ml double cream

Jasmine sugar syrup
200ml water
200g sugar
1 jasmine flower

First make the jasmine syrup, bring the water and sugar to the boil in a pan until the sugar has dissolved. Add a jasmine flower, which will open up and perfume the sugar as it simmers for a further 2 minutes, then remove from the heat and allow the syrup to cool.

Cut the dragon fruit in half lengthways and carefully scoop out the contents keeping the empty casing tidy. Wash any remaining flesh out with water and place in the freezer to harden until needed.

Cut the dragon fruit into cubes, pulp in a blender and sieve to remove the black seeds.

Combine the pulp with the jasmine syrup, coconut water, lime juice and cream in the pre-frozen ice-cream machine and churn for 10 minutes, or until the consistency has thickened. Alternatively, freeze the mixture in a shallow tray, stirring every half an hour with a fork until frozen to sorbet consistency.

Scoop the contents back into the fruit and allow to freeze for at least 1 hour before serving.

Passion and Peach Sorbet in Passion fruit
To fill 2 passion fruits
Flesh of 4 passion fruit
100ml peach juice

Lemongrass infused sugar syrup
1 lemongrass stalk
100g sugar
100ml water

Begin by splitting the lemongrass in quarters, then heat the sugar and water in a pan to simmering point. Add the lemongrass and allow to infuse over the heat for 5 minutes. Strain out the lemongrass and allow the syrup to cool.

Hollow out the passion fruit and place the seeds and golden elixir in a bowl. Stir the peach juice and syrup together, then add the mixture to a pre-frozen ice-cream machine and churn for 10 minutes. Alternatively, freeze the mixture in a shallow tray, stirring every half an hour with a fork until frozen to sorbet consistency.

Spoon the contents back into the fruit halves and allow to freeze for at least an hour before serving.

Serving Suggestion
Arrange all the ice medleys piled up on a large platter, and place them in centre of the table. Add 2 hollowed-out pineapples filled with a rubix of cubed dragon fruit flesh, pineapple and watermelon pieces.

Tutti Frutti Jelly: watch out for the flesh eating enzymes

Tutti Frutti Jelly

By Olivia Bennett of Bompas & Parr
Photography by Ann Charlott Ommedal

The pleasing fruity pastel hues, suspended in a DIY cream soda remind us of the sun drenched seaside pier, filled with fruit machines, creaky ghost trains, a well-loved helter-skelter and shady rock candy salesmen! The recipe comes with a heavy dose of nostalgia – you get the best flavours of childhood parties, jelly and ice cream, in one bite. What foods these morsels be!

This will make a 1 litre jelly perfect for serving 8

Pineapple **jelly**
For pineapple juice
2 pineapples
4 cardamom pods
1 vanilla pod
Pinch of ground cinnamon
1 litre water

For the jelly
130ml sugar syrup (see below)
15ml lime juice
6 gelatine leaves

Guava **jelly**
50ml sugar syrup (see below)
300ml guava Juice
20ml lime juice
4 gelatine leaves

Lime **jelly**
150ml sugar syrup (see below)
250ml lime juice
100ml water
5 gelatine leaves

Cream soda jelly
300 ml sugar syrup (see below)
1 knob of ginger, finely chopped
1 tsp vanilla extract
600ml soda water
50ml ginger beer
30ml lemon juice
1 tsp cream of tartar
200ml Maraschino liqueur
10 gelatine leaves

Begin by making a batch of simple sugar syrup, which can be used for all the fruit jellies. Combine 300g sugar with 600ml boiling water and stir until completely dissolved. (The cream soda sugar syrup should be made separately and infused with chopped fresh ginger and vanilla extract.)

Juice for the fruit jellies – denaturing the enzymes
Some tropical fruits have powerful flesh-eating enzymes. If not denatured while jellying you'll be left with a sticky puddle rather than a proud jelly. Both pineapples and guava fruits need to be dealt with in this way so there's a crucial early stage for this recipe.

Begin by chopping your pineapples into small cubes, and place in a saucepan. To spice the fruit, add the cardamom, the scored and halved vanilla pod, and cinnamon. Finally, cover with the water and cling film the pan. Bring to the boil then reduce the heat and simmer for 15 minutes to extract the juice. The enzymes in the pineapple will have broken down from this process. Sieve the mixture twice and you will have a clear and fragrant juice to make the jelly. (This will most likely be close to 600ml.)

For the same reason, it is essential to bring the guava juice to the boil and allow it to simmer for 2–4minutes before using, in order to ensure that the enzymes break down.

Universal jelly principal applied to the lime jelly
NOTE: All the pineapple, guava and lime jellies recipes are designed to set slightly firmer than we would normally set a jelly. This allows them to be unmoulded and cut into cubes to suspend within the final cream soda jelly.

Begin by juicing the limes; remember to sieve the lime juice to remove the pulp.

As a rule of thumb, 100ml of jelly should be set with 1 leaf of gelatine. Cut the 6 leaves of gelatine into thumb-width pieces and place in a heatproof bowl. Add a few tablespoons of the jelly mixture so that the gelatine is just covered. Let the gelatine soften for 10 minutes while you bring a small pan of water to a simmer, then place the bowl of softened gelatine over the simmering water and stir from time to time until totally melted.

Pour the remainder of the lime jelly mixture over the melted gelatine and stir to combine. Finally, pour the mixture through a sieve into a jug. Fill a loaf cake tin or similar to a depth of 0.5cm and place in the fridge. When set, unmould the jelly using a bath of lukewarm water, then cut into even cubes.

Repeat this process for both the Pineapple and Guava recipes using the juices prepared as above.

Cream Soda Jelly
Start by making DIY cream soda. Infuse a fresh batch of sugar syrup (300ml) with chopped ginger and the vanilla pod: bring them to the boil in a saucepan and allow the sugar syrup to thicken slightly; this will provide a good

background note. Make up with soda water, lemon juice and ginger beer to taste. Add the cream of tartar for extra fizz, and the Maraschino liqueur for a cherry kick. The Maraschino adds a warming cherry hit and is a classic flavour component of fruit salads.

If you use a shop-bought version of cream soda, add half the quantity of sugar syrup mentioned and the full amount of lemon. We recommend Marks & Spencer or Barr's Original which has a hint of raspberry.

Cut the gelatine leaves required again working to 1 leaf per 100ml. Soften and then melt the leaves in a pan over a low heat, as in all previous recipes. When melted, sieve and add back to the cream soda liquid. Allow this to cool, almost (but not quite) setting to a loose consistency. To speed this up you can stir the mixture rapidly in a metal bowl over another bowl filled with ice.

Once the cream soda jelly has almost set, get out the three types of super fruity jelly cubes, green, pink and yellow. You will have to move quickly. Choose a wide, 1-litre mould, gradually incorporate a mix of coloured cubes into the cream soda jelly; they should remain suspended in it. Gradually pour into the mould. You may prefer to add the cubes and cream soda alternately to build the colours, but ensure that there are no large air bubbles in the mixture. This will prevent the jelly setting as a whole.

Allow to set in the fridge for at least 4 hours before unmoulding to serve.

Food as Spectacle – The Tropical Trifle

By Sam Bompas
Photography by Ann Charlott Ommedal

Since the dawn of history there have been only three, truly great, dining spectacles.

The first was Herny VIII's 1521 Garter banquet where jellies were served for both the first and second course. The second was Bartolomeo Scappi's feast for Pope Pius V where the table was arranged as a fishpond composed entirely of comestibles. Small song birds were hidden in the specially folded napkins and released with a flutter of chirrups as the guests tied them round their necks.

The third and greatest by far, belonged to George IV, when he hosted the last proper British meal held in the Renaissance style. For his coronation banquet in 1821 the overweight sybarite, connoisseur and patron of the arts wished to ape the original ceremony of James II.

The tables took two hours to lay, featured 336 silver plates, a sideboard display of solid gold crockery and were illuminated by almost 2000 candles. This was food as a spectator sport with crowds invited to watch the feast being consumed from the galleries

The dinner kicked off when the Hereditary Champion rode a horse into the hall in full armour and threw down his gauntlet challenging anyone to deny the new sovereign. With no-one taking up the challenge the full retinue saluted each other with hearty toasts and set into the food – an assault course of a menu. They ate their way through braised hams, turtle soup, assorted pies, daubed geese, lobster, cold roast fowl, jellies (of course) and over a thousand side dishes. Nearly five hundred sauceboats, brimming over with lobster sauce, butter sauce and mint, lubed the dishes.

While the guests sitting at table feasted, hunger dominated the galleries as many hadn't eaten since breakfast. The frustrations of watching their relatives gorge could only have increased the desire to eat. One peer is said to have wrapped a capon in his napkin and thrown it to his family who were watching in the galleries.

After the King, a noted gourmand, had fed off eight different types of animal he and his retinue left Westminster Hall. At which point, it got feral. The spectators fell upon the spoils, setting out to pillage the table in a savage and unfettered rout.

'The gathering crowds of spoliators, by a simultaneous rush, in a moment surrounded the royal table. For a few seconds delicacy, or a disinclination to be the first to commence the scene of plunder, suspended the projected attack: but at last a rude hand having been thrust through the first ranks, and a golden fork having been seized, this operated as a signal to all, and was followed by a general snatch … The Lord Great Chamberlain managed to rescue the large plate so plunder was confined to small items and inexpensive plates and items … The scene which now presented scarce admits of parallel in modern times.'

Indeed … Thankfully this fruit trifle is so substantial it can withstand several appetite driven attacks.

Passion fruit jelly
50ml sugar syrup
400ml medium white wine
50ml Kirsch
A squeeze of lime juice
3 passion fruit (juiced and seeds held)
5 gelatine leaves
food colour to desired orange

Make the sugar syrup by combining 50g sugar and 50ml boiling water and stirring until the sugar has dissolved. Set aside to cool.

Tropical trifle, a dish so substantial it can withstand several appetite driven attacks

Tutti   •   Frutti

Combine all the ingredients apart from the passion fruit seeds and set using the gelatine leaves. For jelly making tips see the Tutti Frutti jelly recipe on page 55.

The only trick with this is setting the passion fruit seeds beautifully in the jelly. To do this, you need to almost gel the mixture before putting it in the fridge to set. This will suspend the passion fruit seeds evenly throughout the jelly for full visual impact.

Set the bowl of jelly mixture over a larger bowl filled with iced water. Stir in the passion fruit seeds and continue stirring until the mixture is sufficiently gelled that the seeds do not sink to the bottom.

Pour the jelly into 10 small moulds and place in the fridge to set.

For the coconut whipped cream
120ml double cream
50g caster sugar
50ml coconut milk

Whip the double cream and sugar using a food mixer or a hand-held electric whisk. Mix in the coconut milk. Refrigerate until needed.

For the orange custard
8 egg yolks
50g caster sugar
2 tsp cornflour
600ml double cream
Juice of 1 large orange

In a heatproof bowl, whisk the egg yolks with the sugar and cornflour. Heat the cream until it is scalding then pour over the egg yolks, stirring vigorously as you do so. Add the orange juice and pour back into the bowl, then place over a pan of simmering water. Stir until it thickens, then allow to cool. Once cool, refrigerate.

For the pineapple and lime jam
2 medium-sized pineapples
granulated sugar
juice of 2 limes

Peel, core and eye the pineapples then chop finely, trying to save as much of the juice as possible. Have a bowl ready on the scales, weigh the chopped pineapple and add an equal quantity of sugar, then add the lime juice. Cover with cling film and refrigerate overnight.

Transfer the sugary fruit to a pan and boil rapidly until a set is achieved. You can add extra pectin if this is taking too long. Use a refrigerator cold plate to test it.

Lady fingers
These are essential. You can pick up a workhorse version from most supermarkets or follow our very own recipe in *Feasting with Bompas & Parr*.

To decorate
Chop up whatever fruit you can get your hands on to stud the top of the trifle.

Almonds in geometric patterns are grand.

In the past we've favoured a pineapple top studded with cigarettes (held on with cocktail sticks).

To assemble the trifle
Find the mightiest trifle dish at your disposal. Glass is best as it gives you a geological cross section through the trifle so you can see the sugary strata. Begin by layering in the lady fingers along the bottom and sides, sprinkling with Kirsch as you go, then spoon in half the jam trying to spread it evenly over the biscuits. Next, add half the custard and then half the whipped cream. Repeat with more jam, then custard, finishing with a big mound of cream on top. Place your chopped tropical fruit, and whatever other decoration is appropriate, on top. Unmould the jellies and place them around the circumference of the trifle dish. Let the spectacle commence.

Fruit Ice Lollies

By Bompas & Parr. Photography by Nathan Pask

The tongue is one of the best organs at healing itself in the body. Unlike other organs it can heal when wet. Even if you split your tongue to create a devilish forked tongue, primary healing (where you can talk and eat relatively normally) takes only one or two weeks.

Though we do some pretty extreme things to our tongues (hot drinks, ices) we need it to be fit enough to taste and alert us to potential poisons. It is constantly regenerating itself. The average life for a taste bud is only 10 days so within a month your entire taste apparatus is refreshed.

Marinade on this as you attentively lick your fruit ice.

You will need store bought plastic lolly moulds to make these fellows.

For 6–8 ice lollies

Lolly base
900g caster sugar
1 litre boiling water
6 lemons
100ml orange juice

A Fruit Ice Lolly; refreshing the entire taste apparatus

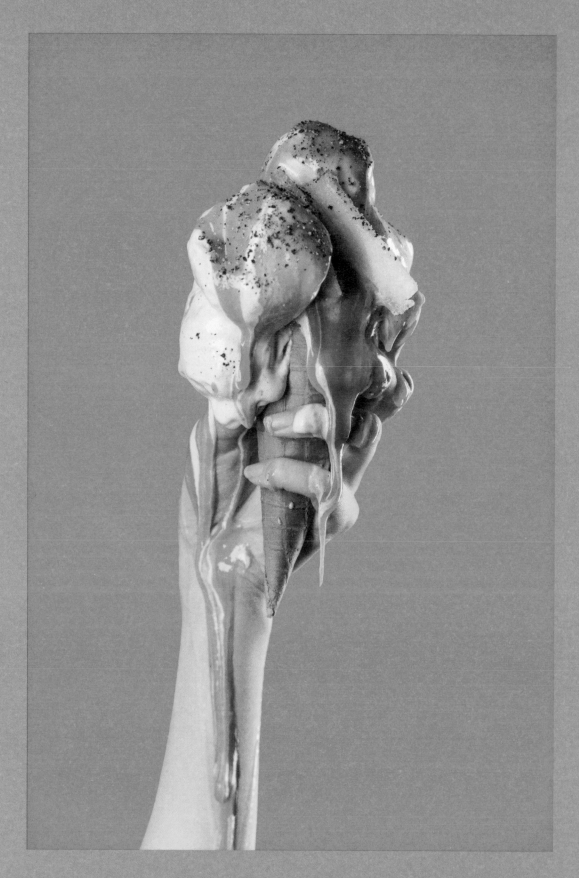

"Don't be frightened"
Florence Knight

Fresh Fruits
1 blood orange, peeled and sliced
4 strawberries
1 peach, stoned and sliced
8 blueberries
8 raspberries

Begin by making a simple syrup with the sugar and boiling water. Allow to simmer in a saucepan over the heat until completely dissolved, then allow to cool. Juice 6 lemons to get roughly 130ml of fresh lemon juice, and add 100ml orange juice. Combine this with the sugar syrup for your lolly base.

Now select the fresh fruits for your lolly. We recommend a slice of blood orange, strawberry, peach, blueberry and fresh raspberry goes into each 150ml ice. Carefully place the first of the fresh fruit slices in a lolly mould, say the blueberry, raspberry and blood orange then fill hallway up the mould with the lolly juice mixture.

Allow to freeze for 30 minutes. Remove from the freezer, and add the peach slice and strawberry.

To complete the lolly, fill to the top with the more lolly juice liquid and insert the stick. The pre-frozen lolly part should make keeping the stick in the middle a little easier. Place back in the freezer and allow to freeze for a further 2 hours before serving.

Peppered Ice Cream,
Pineapple & Toffee

By Florence Knight. Photography by Nathan Pask

I like to celebrate forgotten combinations in my cooking. Pepper was the original spice and was used in all manner of ways when it was first brought back from the East Indies, but nowadays it's more or less just a simple sprinkle or scatter at the end of cooking. I think there's more to it than that.

Don't be frightened, the cracked pepper works beautifully with the perfumed sweetness of the pineapple. It adds depth and heat to what could otherwise be sickly sweet.

As it happens, I rarely cook with tropical ingredients as I try not to wander too far away from locally grown produce, but I can never resist the glorious tufty pineapple. I'm not alone either: it has been travelling across the seas to England for centuries and has traditionally been used as a symbol of fertility and plenty but I think the pineapple's popularity really lies in the fact that it's just truly delicious.

Please don't compromise on the quality of the fruit. Ripeness is key. You can tell a pineapple is ripe by its colour and its smell. If the pineapple is slightly yellow and smells sweet then it's ready to eat. If it's too green then you should turn it upside down for a few days – this generally does the trick.

This is a simple dessert but one that will surprise and challenge you a little.

Serves 8

Ice Cream
1 vanilla pod
125ml whole milk
750ml double cream
10 free-range egg yolks
175g caster sugar
1 tbsp cracked black pepper
1 ripe pineapple

Toffee sauce
50g unsalted butter
125g light muscovado sugar
150g golden syrup
1 x 170g can evaporated milk

Run a knife down the centre of the vanilla pod and extract the seeds. Add both the seeds and pod to a heavy-based pan. Pour over the milk and cream then place the pan over a medium heat, bringing it to just below boiling point.

In a large bowl, whisk the yolks and sugar until they're light and hold a ribbon in the froth. Pour the milk and cream little by little over the fluffy yolks, stirring continuously. Return this to the pan and simmer gently, keep stirring to stop the mixture turning into scrambled egg.

When the mixture coats the back of the spoon; I run my finger along the back to see that a line stays – if it does, it is ready. Remove from the heat and strain it through a fine sieve into a large bowl. Cover with the cling film directly on the surface of the cream so that it doesn't form a skin. Leave the mixture to cool in the fridge.

Once cold, pour the mixture into an ice-cream machine and churn until soft set, then scatter over the pepper and let the ice-cream machine churn until frozen. Alternatively, freeze the mixture in a shallow tray, stirring every half an hour and adding a little of the pepper each time until set.

While waiting for the ice cream to set you can start to make the toffee sauce. Place the butter, sugar and syrup into a medium pan and heat gently, stirring continuously until the sugar has dissolved into the butter and melted into a thick liquid. Bring the syrupy mixture to a gentle simmer for 8 minutes. Don't be temped to stop stirring, as the mixture will stick to the base of the pan.

Remove the pan from the heat and gradually pour in the evaporated milk. Warm through the sauce over a low heat and combine everything together with a good stir and set it aside.

Take the pineapple and cut or pull the leaves out from the top of the fruit, then using a sharp knife, cut the base off so you have a stable surface. Gently plonk the pineapple on its even bottom. Using a fruit knife, slice the peel in a downwards direction using a sawing motion to remove it, working your way round the whole fruit. Remove any 'eyes' (the little tufty bits) by cutting small 'v' shaped grooves diagonally down either side working your way around the pineapple.

Using a mandolin or very sharp knife, slice paper-thin slivers of pineapple. Layer and drape them over a ball of the ice cream and pour over a little of the warm toffee sauce.

Tutti-Frutti Bombe

By Sam Bompas

The term Tutti-Frutti is Italian, meaning 'all the fruits'. It's used to describe a whole landscape of different desserts that combine several fruity flavours and are studded with a kaleidoscope of chopped, poached, candied, crystallised and stylishly prepared little fruit pieces.

Visit Italy to find Tutti Frutti ice creams, pastries and sweets. Curiously Tutti Frutti is also a European 'erotic TV show' from the late 1980s and early '90s where pneumatic contestants and stripping formed the greater part of the entertainment. Initially it was pretty successful – largely due to the 'ragazze cin cin' – a group of glamour models and former playmates who each represented a specific fruit and filled special roles on the show. Some are still known as their fruit based names.

Though tawdry, the game show was innovative in pioneering early 3D technology. By scrolling a background across the screen at a slower speed than the dancers in the foreground, the Pulfrich effect gave the effect of depth on a 2D screen. The idea was to 'bring to life' the nubile gyrations of the fruity hosts and subjects.

Here's a suitably suggestive version of the dessert. Let's get sticky!

Serves 8

Ingredients
1 litre pineapple ice cream
250g caster sugar
100ml water
8 egg yolks
1 tbsp Kirsch
400g candied fruits
100g raisins soaked in rum and drained well
Assorted glacé cherries, candied angelica and almonds

Chantilly Cream
50g icing sugar
250ml whiping cream

Line a bombe mould with the ice cream and put in the freezer to harden.

Make the Chantilly cream by combining the icing sugar with the cream. Using a hand balloon whisk or electric whisk, beat the cream in a stainless steel or glass or china bowl (not plastic – doesn't seem to whip as well). It is whipped properly when it is still soft and billowy but holds its shape when the whisk is withdrawn. Once the cream is whipped, cover and store in the fridge until needed. If it separates slightly, just rewhip to restore its thickness.

Make a sugar syrup by bringing the water to the boil, taking off the heat and stirring in the sugar until it is totally dissolved. Now place the saucepan in a bain-marie/water bath and blend in 8 egg yolks. Whisk on a hob until frothy, then strain and whisk once more in a basin.

Mix in the Chantilly cream, Kirsch, candied fruits and raisins, then pour into the mould and freeze for 4 hours.

Once you unmould, stud the bomb with candied cherries, angelica and almonds each chopped down to your own design. We like to take inspiration for our decoration from architecture or anatomy depending on mood, weather and whom we are serving it to. Breast or dome, it's up to you.

Behold. In tribute to the Pulfrich effect we've made a movie of the Tutti Frutti Bombe that you can see in titillating 3D online at Bompas & Parr's website.

All you need is a pair of sunglasses. Load up the film, step back from your screen and look through a single lens of the sunglasses. There are two effective ways to do this. Either wear them jocularly on the slant or pop one lens out of the frame. Marvel as the bombe pulsates, gyrates and jumps right out of the screen at you.

Fruit and Flora Ice Cream Sundae

By Wayward Plants
Photography by Ann Charlott Ommedal

The first time we transformed a vacant lot into an orchard, filled with fruit trees and hedges of berries, we made sure to pick our fair share of apples come harvest. Of course, we didn't realise at the time that the apple blossoms were edible as well. With a subtle floral taste, the apple blossoms must be eaten delicately and with caution, for the seeds contain a precursor to cyanide, which gets released during digestion. So, a little bit might taste sweet, but a bit too much and you may get sick.

The prospect of devising a unique fruit salad was intriguing to us, especially from a botanical standpoint. After all, there are a plethora of flavours held in the birthplace of fruit: the flower. Soon we were sipping orange blossom cordials whilst concocting the perfect summer dessert: our Fruit and Flora Ice Cream Sundae – a delectable mixture of floral and fruity ice creams, sorbets, syrups and foams, topped with a bouquet of crystallised petals.

Combine the subtle, aromatic flavour of the rose sorbet with the spicy sweetness of the lavender ice cream. Pour orange blossom syrup generously over the top, add a foam of apple and elderflowers and sprinkle on a healthy handful of frosted pansy petals and seasonal berries. We suggest serving this ice cream garden in a bowl of ice, filled with frozen flowers. All these ice creams and sorbets, syrups, foams and frosted flowers can be adapted to create all manner of combinations – you can replace our suggestions with whichever edible flowers and fruit are available and in season.

A Word of Warning

Edible flowers can be found in speciality shops and farmers markets or you can grow your own – however, avoid getting them from flower shops. Be sure that the flowers you choose are organically home-grown and free of pesticides.

Generally, make sure you only eat the petals, not the stems, pistil or leaves. If you suffer from any allergy to pollen, such as hay fever, we strongly recommend that you do not follow this recipe (for all the obvious reasons, do so at your own risk). Finally, for the removal of any doubt, ensure that the flowers you choose are safe to eat – whilst there is a long list of edible flowers, there is an equally long list of poisonous ones.

Bases

Rose Sorbet

1 very large handful of rose petals
400ml water
125g caster sugar
a drop of lemon juice
½ egg white (optional)

Separate the rose petals from the flowerhead and chop off the white base. Chop the petals finely.

Bring the water and sugar to the boil in a saucepan and add a drop of lemon juice. Reduce the heat, add the rose petals and simmer for 5 minutes. Strain through a fine sieve and refrigerate.

If using an ice-cream machine, add the egg white. As you churn the sorbet, the egg white will trap millions of tiny air bubbles in the mixture making your sorbet as white as meringue. Churn until hard and then serve. Alternatively, forget the egg white and add the ingredients to a freezerproof bowl and place this in a freezer. Whisk the mixture every 5 minutes, thereby helping to break up the ice crystals and create a smoother mix. The sorbet can be left alone after (approximately) 30 minutes, and can be eaten after about 4 hours.

Lavender ice cream

8 large egg yolks
250g sugar
2 teaspoons vanilla extract
¼ tsp salt
1 can evaporated milk
1 large handful of lavender flowers, plus a bunch
500ml double cream

In a large bowl or mixer, whisk the egg yolks, sugar, vanilla and salt until the mixture turns light and pale yellow. Set aside.

Heat the evaporated milk and lavender in a medium saucepan until it comes to a simmer, then set this aside for 5 minutes.

Using a sieve to remove the lavender, slowly add the warm milk to the egg mixture, whisking constantly. Transfer the mixture back to the pan and heat, continuing to whisk, bringing it up to 80°C (it should become thick and custardy). Don't overheat or the eggs will scramble. Chill the mixture completely in the fridge.

Whisk your first 250ml of double cream until you are left with soft peaks. Add this to the egg mixture and fold it in gently until there are no lumps remaining. Pour the mixture into ice-cube trays and freeze for 4 hours, or until solid.

Combine the frozen cubes of ice cream and the remaining double cream in a food processor and process

The floral ice bowl has many life enhancing applications

until a smooth mixture is produced. Place the mix in a shatterproof container, slowly folding in a bunch of whole lavender flowers, and freeze for at least another 4 hours.

Toppings

Orange Blossom Syrup
250g granulated sugar
250ml water
1 large handful of orange blossoms

In a heavy-based pan, bring the sugar and water to the boil over a medium-high heat. Add the orange blossoms and keep stirring for another few minutes before removing the pan from the heat. Allow the mixture to cool completely. Pour the syrup through a fine mesh sieve into a container with a fitted lid. Use this delicate syrup in moderate amounts.

Apple and Elderflower Foam
200ml apple juice of your choice (chilled)
2.4g powdered gelatine
Elderflower cordial to taste
Fresh lemon juice to taste
Caster sugar to taste
Salt to taste

Pour 20ml of the apple juice into a shallow dish with the gelatine. After a few minutes the gelatine will soften, at which point you should warm the mixture over a low heat until all the gelatine has melted. Then, pour in the remaining apple juice and, once combined, add the other ingredients to taste. The result should not be subtle; rather, it should be strongly flavoured to create a tasty foam. Carefully, pour the resulting liquid into a whipping siphon loaded with the required number of nitrous oxide cartridges. To ensure the best results, chill the liquid inside the siphon for several hours before serving. While serving, hold the siphon upside down.

This recipe can be adapted to incorporate almost any fruit juice and/or floral syrup.

Frosted Pansies
1 handful of pansies or any other chosen
(edible) flowers, leaves or petals
1 egg white
2 tbsp caster sugar

Remove all stalks and green parts, along with any stamens from the pansies. Lightly beat the egg white. Hold the flower, petal or leaf at the base and, using a small brush, paint with egg white (front and back). Lightly sprinkle the saster sugar over the petals (front and back), which will cling to the moist surface. Taking care to retain the shape as much as possible, place the flowers on parchment paper on a plate or wire rack and keep them in a warm place until they become crisp and dry. Store the flowers in an airtight tin or jar. They can be kept for two days.

Assorted Seasonal Berries
Top the sundae with blackberries, strawberries, blueberries and raspberries, loganberries, pineberries (a strawberry that tastes like pineapple) and even miracle berries (a berry that will turn your whole sundae savoury).

Presentation
Ice Bowl (for serving)

Scatter roses, buds, small flowers and sprigs of leaves, such as mint, in the base of a large bowl. Weigh them down with plenty of ice cubes.

Rest a medium-sized bowl over the ice cubes inside the large bowl – so that it sits in the centre, creating an even air space between the two bowls. Pour cold water between the bowls until the water rises 4cm up the sides. Weight the centre bowl and place it in a freezer.

After 2 to 3 hours, remove the bowls from the freezer and their weights. Tuck more flowers, petals and leaves between the bowls and top up to 5mm from the rim with water. Freeze overnight until solid. Remove from the freezer and leave on a counter for 5 minutes. Then, immerse both bowls in boiling water and let them stand for a few seconds. Remove and release the lower bowl. To remove the upper bowl, fill this with boiling water, then twist and release!

BAKING &
PRESERVING

ADDRESSING THE
ALVINE NEED

#005

Lithia Log (Midsummer fruit log)

By Harry Parr

Ancient druids knew how to drink. They also knew a good way to celebrate midsummer, the longest day of the year and an important festival in the pre-Christian calendar.

In pagan days, people across Europe would mark the significant date with strange and arcane rituals. In what has become Hungary, girls would jump over lit bonfires, in France cats would be burnt and in England the mysterious Stonehenge is said to have had a special significance.

While specific customs around the celebration of midsummer may have varied, total merriment, dancing and all night drinking remained the universal theme. The festival was effectively a pan-European mega party, as folk across the northern hemisphere celebrated the solstice, lit fires and got drunk at the same time.

Celebrate for yourself with our tasty Lithia log. It's the fruity midsummer cousin of the dusky Yule log that may be forced on you at Christmas. The dessert makes best use of the first strawberries of the season and is a symbol of summer potency in its own right.

Offer ecstatic libations to the sun as you plate this dish with clumps of cream and have a sweet cider on the side, the drink of druids.

Don't just stare at it, eat it!

Serves 8

Cake
3 large eggs
75g caster sugar (split into 25g and 50g)
75g self-raising flour

Filling
125ml whipped double cream
a few strawberries
75g cherry jam (or other fruit jam)

Icing
150g unsalted butter
300g icing sugar
a splash of milk (optional)

To Serve
strawberries, blackberries, raspberries
whipped double cream

Preheat the oven to 180°C/350°F/Gas mark 4 and grease and line a 24 x 36cm shallow tin.

Separate the eggs, placing both the yolks and whites into large mixing bowls. Start by whisking the yolks with 25g of sugar until the mixture is pale and fluffy. Carefully wash the beaters so that no traces of yolk remain. Whisk the whites, gradually adding the rest of the sugar, and continue beating until the mixture is thick and glossy, about 2 minutes.

Add a spoonful of the whites to the yolks and gentle whisk in. Add the rest of the whites and whisk very briefly until they are just combined. Add the flour in three stages, whisking briefly after each addition.

Pour the mixture into the prepared tin and bake in the oven for about 12 minutes. When pressed the surface should be slightly elastic and spring back. Place a piece of greaseproof paper onto a wire rack, then turn the lot upside down, place on top of the cake, and invert. Carefully peel the greaseproof paper from the cake and allow to cool.

For the filling, spread the jam thinly over the cake. Whip the cream then spread the cream into a 5cm wide channel down the length of the cake. Thinly slice the strawberries and place in one layer on the cream. Trim 1cm or so from the edge of the cake, then roll the cake lengthways. Wrap in the greaseproof paper and leave in the fridge until ready to ice.

For the icing, cut the butter into cubes and beat until soft, then gradually add the icing sugar until it is all incorporated. If the mixture is too stiff add a splash of milk. Cut off one end of the log at 45 degrees, using it to create a branch stub. Arrange the cake on a serving plate and use the icing to sculpt a realistic looking branch. Arrange the berries around the log and serve with extra whipped cream.

Bottled (Embalmed) Fruit Salad

By Sam Bompas

You can make your very own fruit salad that can be served straight from the jar to excited guests. The trick is to preserve your favourite fruits from the cruelties of bacteria, fungus and decay in a sugar syrup. This gives your precious fruit a mysteriously extended life. With an hour or so of fruiting you can wave goodbye to Del Monte's canned fruit salad forever.

You are effectively embalming your fruit, killing the existing bacteria with heat and using sugar to reduce the available water that future bacteria need to breed.

Use any fruits you like save for bananas which ferment and fizz. Be wary of dark-skinned fruits which could stain the rest of your concoction. It's worth experimenting to see what works for your experienced palate.

The bottled fruits can be beautiful and will make for excellent and luxurious gifts. Marvel as the grapes, plums, pears and peaches escape the ravages of time just liked embalmed celebrities Eva Perón of Argentina, Vladimir Lenin of Russia and Pope John XXIII.

Fills around six 1kg jars

Fruit Salad
1.25kg plums
600g small seedless green grapes
12 ripe peaches
1.25kg ripe pears
chilled cream, to serve

Ambrosial Embalming Fluid
1.75 litres water
1kg granulated sugar
Peel of 1 orange, chopped into fine slivers
Peel of 1 lemon, chopped into fine slivers

6 glass jars with lids each approx 1 litre in volume

Compose your sugar syrup for the ambrosial embalming fluid by bringing the water to the boil in a pan and stirring in all the sugar until it has totally dissolved, then removing the pan from the heat and setting aside.

Prep your fruit by washing the plums and stoning them.

Deseeding the grapes and halving them if they are particularly large.

Skinning the peaches by plunging them in boiling water for 30 seconds before draining and placing in cold water. Work with your hands underwater to remove the skins. Now you can halve the peaches and get rid of the stone.

Coring and quartering the pears.

As each batch of fruit is prepared keep them in cool water to stop the flesh going brown.

Preheat the oven to 180°C/350°F/Gas mark 4. Mix up all the fruit and distribute between the glass jars. Stand the jars on a baking tray lined with newspaper and make sure they aren't touching.

Heat the sugar syrup once more so it's boiling and fill each of the jars to the brim, totally submerging the fruit. Place the lids on top (without screwing them down). Heat in the oven for 1 hour. This will cook the fruit and sterilise the glass simultaneously.

Use a clean dishtowel or a pair of oven gloves to take the tray out of the oven and screw on the lids. Now let the jars totally cool and store until you can resist no longer. The results are DROOLWORTHY!

Serve with a spoonful of chilled cream. Nothing else is needed.

Jewelled Fruit Doughnut Obelisk of Deception

By Justin Piers Gellatly of St John
Photography by Nathan Pask

The doughnuts have become a large part at St John Bakery, it's a recipe which took me around 50 different goes to get right, with issues with the sweetness, and how much butter to use, but the main problem was the yeast amount; yes we did have exploding doughnuts! The doughnut obelisk is like a fruit salad, just the fruit is encased in doughnuts.

Makes 90 doughnuts

Doughnut dough
1kg strong white flour
125g caster sugar
20g fine sea salt
30g fresh yeast
8 eggs
2 lemons zested
300ml water
250g unsalted butter, softened
Rapeseed oil, for frying

Glaze
1.2kg icing sugar
250g milk + a little more up your sleeve

Fillings
8 kiwi fruit
300g blueberries
300g blackberries
4 sticks rhubarb
30 strawberries
5 oranges
1 pineapple
6 bananas

Additional ingredients included below

Coloured sugars
60g granulated sugar per 6–8 drops of food colouring per each sugar. Colours – yellow, orange, red, green, blue, pink and purple.

To make each sugar, place 60g of sugar into a jar with a tight-fitting lid. Drip the food colouring onto the sugar, then close the lid and shake vigorously for about 2–3 minutes. Adjust colour with additional food colouring if it's not dark enough.

For the dough
Place all the ingredients except the butter and oil in the bowl of a food mixer. Mix on a medium speed for 6 minutes, then scrape down the sides of the bowl. Start mixing on medium speed again, adding the soft butter, about 20g at a time until all incorporated. Keep mixing for 6–8 minutes until the dough has come away from the sides of the bowl and looks glossy and elastic.

Place the dough in a large bowl, sprinkle the surface with flour and cover the bowl with a tea towel.

The Jewelled Fruit Doughnut Obelisk of Deception in full splendor. Don't just stare at it, eat it!

Leave to rise for 2–3 hours in warm place until doubled in size. Knock back the dough, then cover the bowl with cling film and place in the fridge for at least 4 hours or overnight.

Cut the dough into 20g pieces and roll them into smooth balls. Place on floured baking trays, leaving about 3cm between each one. Cover with cling film and leave to prove for 2–3 hours; depending on how warm it is; they should double in size.

Half-fill a deep-fat fryer or a deep, heavy-based saucepan with the oil and heat to 180°C/350°F. The temperature is very important, too high and the doughnuts will burn and too low they will absorb the oil making them greasy.

With the oil at the correct temperature, start frying the doughnuts in batches of 7–8 at a time, until golden brown. They will take about 2 minutes each side. Remember to check the temperature of the oil between each batch. As the doughnuts are done, place them on kitchen paper to soak up the excess oil.

Make the glaze. Whisk the sugar and milk in a large bowl until smooth and honey-like. Spread the coloured sugars onto plates. Dip the doughnuts into the glaze, place on a wire rack and leave to stand for about 1 minute until the excess has dripped off but the glaze is still wet. Then toss them in the coloured sugars.

Now for the fillings

Kiwi fruit
Peel and chop finely the kiwi fruit so you can pipe it.

Blueberries
2 tbsp jam sugar
1 tbsp cornflour

Place the berries in a pan with the jam sugar and bring to a light simmer, then whisk in the cornflour mixed to a paste with a few drops of water. Bring back to the boil, then take off the heat and whisk. Chill and place in a piping bag.

Blackberries
This is the same method as above.

Rhubarb
500ml water
400g caster sugar
4 tbsp rhubarb jam

Finely dice the rhubarb and place it in a metal bowl. Bring the water and caster sugar to the boil in a pan, reduce the heat and simmer for 3–4 minutes. Pour over the rhubarb then cover tightly with cling film and leave to cool.

Strain the rhubarb, mix with the rhubarb jam and place in a piping bag. Set aside.

Strawberries
Hull and finely dice the strawberries then place in a piping bag. Set aside.

Orange
juice of 2 lemons
finely grated and juice of 4 oranges
200g unsalted butter
400g caster sugar
6 eggs, beaten

Place the lemon juice, orange juice and grated zest in a large heatproof bowl with the butter and sugar; set the bowl over a saucepan of simmering water, making sure the water doesn't touch the base of the bowl. Leave until the butter has melted, then whisk in the beaten eggs. Cook for about 10 minutes whisking every 2–3 minutes until the curd has thickened. Once thick pass through a fine sieve and chill, then place in a piping bag.

Pineapple
Peel and core the pineapple then finely dice and place in a piping bag. Set aside.

Bananas
Peel the bananas, then mush together with the juice of ½ lemon and place in a piping bag. Set aside.

Fill the
Red sugar doughnut with pineapple
Yellow one with strawberry
Orange one with kiwi
Green one with orange
Blue one with rhubarb
Pink one with blueberries
White one with blackberries
Purple one with bananas

To serve
Create an obelisk of carved florist's oasis measuring 10 x 10cm base and 60cm in height. Cover the oasis foam with silver foil and attach it to your serving dish/plate, then pin the doughnuts to the oasis foam stack using cocktail sticks. Decorate with fruit around the base.

The deception is for people to eat with their eyes and the colours will trick them. When they bite into a red doughnut most people will think strawberry and then BANG! It's pineapple.

Laser Floating Islands

By Harry Parr

All the best recipes have stories behind them. If they don't you have to make one up. Laser floating islands have no precedent so to give context and intrigue we dedicate the dish to Dr James Graham, a man we think would approve of the innovative and unusual use of technology in pursuit of gastronomic stimulation and novel sensation.

Dr James Graham (1745–1794) was a medical entrepreneur, quack and pioneer in sex therapy with a genius for spectacle. Having learnt the principles of electricity and magnetism from Benjamin Franklin Graham, he established himself as sex therapist to London Society. Graham thought, since static electricity made hair stand on end, it had the power to make any body part erect and that fluids would spurt more vigorously from charged bodies.

In 1781 Graham built a Temple of Hymen in Shomberg House in Pall Mall filled with equipment for electrically stimulating patrons including the Duchess of Devonshire, Charles James Fox and John Wilkes. Graham even employed a succession of 'Goddesses of Health' to demonstrate a 'cold, glowing, full, liquid, balmy firmness of the genital parts'.

The centrepiece of the Temple was the Celestial Bed, reserved for those able to afford the mighty £50 per night fee. Graham advertised that anyone who rented the bed would be 'blessed with progeny'.

The bed measured twelve by nine feet and could be tilted to achieve the perfect angle for conception. The mattress was filled with 'sweet new wheat or oat straw, mingled with balm, rose leaves, and lavender flowers' as well as the hair from the tails of fine English stallions!

The bed was insulated from the floor by 40 glass rod supports allowing the whole bed to become electrically charged. Aristocratic lovers would generate static electricity and cause corona discharge across the headboard manifesting itself in a faint green glow.

Soft music played and the perfumed air was said to include ether or nitrous oxide. A large mirror was suspended above, and two live turtle doves sat at the apex of the headboard alongside the inscription 'Be fruitful. Multiply and Replenish the Earth'.

Graham's bed was enormously successful and fashionable London flocked to patronise his Temple and hear his titillating and grandiloquent sexual health lectures.

'The daily cold washing of the genitals', for example, would not only 'lock the cock and secure all for the next rencontre', but also much improve the testicular condition from 'relaxed, lank, and pendulous, like the two eyes of a dead sheep dangling in a wet empty calf's bladder' to something akin to 'a couple of steel balls, of a pound apiece, enclosed in a firm purse of uncut Manchester velvet!'

Sadly Graham's spending outpaced his earnings and by 1784 he was forced to sell most of his possessions including the celestial bed. It was lost to the world until our re-creation at Valentine's in the Museum of London in 2011. Build your own Celestial Bed and feast on these sensual and astonishing laser floating islands. If they don't 'give the necessary degree of strength and exertion to the nerves' they will at least wow and perhaps woo anyone you are feeding.

Serves 8

Custard	Islands
4 egg yolks	3 egg whites
25g caster sugar	75g + 25g caster sugar
1 vanilla pod	400ml milk
300ml milk	
300ml double cream	

To serve
150g caster sugar
stewed fruit
(the tartness of rhubarb or gooseberries go well)

Start by making the custard. Whisk the egg yolks with the sugar until pale. Scrape the vanilla seeds into a pan then add the milk and the cream and bring to a simmer. Remove from the heat and allow to infuse. Finish the custard by adding the hot milk to the yolks, whisking and then continuing to cook gently until the custard coats the back of a wooden spoon. It should remain relatively thin.

For the islands, use an electric whisk to whisk the egg whites, gradually incorporating the 75g sugar, and whisk for 2 minutes until the mixture is silky and firm. Warm the milk in a wide saucepan and stir in the remaining sugar. Do not let it boil. Using two dessertspoons, form the meringue into balls and poach gently on the surface of the milk, turning occasionally, for 2 minutes. Don't overcrowd the pan and poach in a few batches if necessary. Place on a wire rack to drain.

Make a caramel by melting the 150g caster sugar in a pan over a medium heat, then continue to cook for about 10 minutes, mixing the sugar occasionally so that the caramel forms evenly.

To serve, place a tablespoon of the stewed fruit in the centre of a shallow bowl, surround with custard and then float the islands on top. Use a spoon to flick laser shards of caramel over the surface of the dish.

You won't be able to control yourself around these Pineapple Chelsea Buns; a treasure for your tongue

Pineapple Chelsea Buns

By Amanda Walker, Head Chef, Kew Royal Botanical Gardens. Photography by Nathan Pask

Here's a recipe from the Head Chef at Kew Amanda Walker. Her bromelain (of or relating to the pineapple) take on the robust and traditional Chelsea Bun, which is so tender and fruity you'll see them in your dreams. It will take all of your iron will to resist eating the whole batch while gazing into the summer's blue sky.

Makes 12 buns

Bread
10g fast action dried yeast
500g baker's/white strong bread flour
60g caster sugar
16g mixed spice
finely grated lemon and orange zest
50g unsalted butter
300–500ml pineapple juice
14g salt
2 egg yolks (for egg wash later)

Custard
200ml milk
Vanilla pod
1 egg
25g cornflour
35g caster sugar

Pineapple jelly
½ fresh pineapple
100g caster sugar
100ml water
30ml rum (more if you want)
1 cardamom pod

For the dough, mix the yeast with a little warm water to dissolve. Place the flour into a mixing bowl and add all the dry ingredients, except the salt. Crumble the butter through the dry ingredients, then make a well and first add the yeast mix, then 300ml of fruit juice and mix. If the dough hasn't come together, add a little more juice. Once the mixture forms a ball of dough, start to knead it on a clean work surface. If the dough is sticking to the surface, you may need to add a little more flour. Ideally work without flour on the surface. Knead for about 6 minutes then rub the salt into the dough and knead until the salt has been worked in completely.

Return the dough to the bowl, cover with a wet clean tea towel and leave in a warm place until the dough has doubled in size.

Meanwhile, make the custard. Bring the milk and vanilla pod to the boil in a pan.

Mix the egg, cornflour and caster sugar together in a large heatproof bowl with a whisk, then pour the hot milk over the egg mix and pour back into the pan. Return to the heat and whisk over a medium heat until thick and big bubbles come to the top. Strain the custard through a fine mesh sieve into a clean bowl, then place on a tray, cover the custard with cling film and cool immediately.When cold, whisk again until shiny.

For the pineapple jelly, finely chop the pineapple (don't use the woody core) and place in a pan with the sugar, water, rum and cardamom. Bring to the boil and then cook to reduce the liquid and get a jam-like consistency. Leave to cool down before using.

Bringing it all together: Divide your dough into three, so it's easy to work with. Roll out your dough using a rolling pin until it's around 60cm long and 25cm wide (the dough will be very thin), you also don't want to use flour for this step.

Spread a very thin layer of custard over the dough, then do the same with the jelly. Roll up the dough lengthways, then cut into four (about 5cm) rounds and sit on a baking tray cut side up and spaced well apart. Repeat with the two more pieces of dough and leave to prove in a warm place until the scrolls double in size.

Preheat the oven to 200°C/fan oven 180°C/400°F/Gas mark 6 and bake the buns for 10 minutes. Take out of the oven and brush with the egg wash. Return to the oven and bake for a further 10 minutes. Immediately transfer the buns to a wire rack and cool. Eat while still warm.

TwoTea FruitTea AffogaTea

By Henrietta Lovell of the Rare Tea Company

You may have been bamboozled, fooled and worse still utterly disappointed by drinks masquerading as 'Fruit Tea'. What is usually called fruit tea isn't much in the way of fruit or tea. What's stuffed in a bag is almost never tea (Camellia sinensis) and the fruit is almost always a synthetic flavouring. Sometimes you get the odd floater of dried apple but it's there for its sugar content rather than flavour.

We tend to drink fruit tea because we think it might be good for us. Maybe chemical goops swimming in hot water are good, but I have an idea that fruit and tea might be better.

Even though I'm the tea lady I do love coffee (and gin and whisky and everything that tastes delicious). A few years ago I discovered that coffee baristas – the tattooed, skinny-fit, coffee geeks with their aero presses and ceramic grinders – make very good tea. With a little nudge they can get excited about leaf to water ratios, temperatures and single estate leaves. It was working with them to make an espresso tea that inspired my Two Tea Fruit Tea AffogaTea.

I had started dabbling with re-inventing fruit tea and then came fruit salads with tea. Have you ever tried an affogato: hot espresso poured over ice cream? The strong, rich, coffee is hot and bitter and the ice cream is cold, smooth and sweet. Why not make it with an espresso tea? Here it is, one of the headiest pleasures you will have tasted, ever. Trust me. I'm the tea lady.

Ingredients – For each person
3 ripe, red strawberries, hulled and quartered
1 dark, ripe plum, stoned and sliced
4 mulberries (optional)
30ml damson gin, optional but encouraged
2 scoops of vanilla ice cream
2g (1 teaspoon) Rare Earl Grey Tea*
2g English Breakfast (I would use my Royal Air Force Blend, but I would)
30ml boiling water
3 little fresh mint leaves, to decorate
(use the tender leaves at the top of the sprig)

Put the fruit into the bottom of a teacup or small bowl and pour over the gin if you're using it. Scoop the ice cream on top of the fruit.

Put the tea in a teapot. Measure exactly 30ml of freshly boiled water into the pot and infuse for 1 minute.

While the tea is brewing pour some hot water into a small jug or espresso cup to warm; throw the water away when the tea is infused. Pour the tea into the small jug or espresso cup, then pour the hot tea over the fruit salad just as you are ready to eat, and decorate with the mint.

*You could use a lesser Earl Grey tea but you'll be heading back into the realms of synthetic flavours and away from fruit. Almost all Earl Grey tea is made with bergamot flavouring – I go to Calabria in Southern Italy to find ancient bergamot trees. Bergamot is a citrus fruit – a naturally occurring hybrid of a bitter orange and lemon. We use the essential oil from the zest of the fruit.

Inside Voices

By Thor Bergquist of ECC

Inspired by a culinary trip to Copenhagen, Denmark and the very special cafe 42 Raw, which uses a lot of fresh, raw foods and focuses on dehydrating fruit at low temperatures to intensify their flavours.

Serves 1

Ingredients
50ml blanco tequila infused with dried strawberries
20ml freshly pressed lemon juice
20ml green apple and fennel syrup
5–6 fresh mint leaves
3 dashes Thai chilli tincture
Dried strawberries, to serve

Combine all the ingredients in a Boston shaker, and shake vigorously until frosted (condensation on the outside).

Strain the mixture through a fine sieve into a chilled coupette glass and adorn with dried strawberries to serve.

How to make the ingredients
250g strawberries
1 bottle of blanco tequila
2 green apples (approximately 150g each)
1 fennel bulb (approximately 100g)
500g caster sugar
500ml water
200g red bird's eye chillies
1 bottle of overproof rum

The tequila infusion is made by dehydrating 250g of thinly sliced strawberries for 6 hours at 40°C, then leaving them to infuse in a bottle of Tequila for 6 hours. We use a dehydrator to dry the strawberries but very low heat for 4 hours will also work.

To make the green apple and fennel syrup, peel the apples, save the skin, then chop the fennel and combine the fennel, green apple skin, caster sugar and water in a saucepan. Bring to the boil, then remove from the heat and leave to infuse for 1 hour. Strain.

The Thai chilli tincture is made by slicing 200g red bird's eye chillies and leaving them in a bottle of over-proof rum for 24 hours.

The Brittany – Vodka & Soda

By Sam Bompas. Photography by Nathan Pask

Vodka and water as a cocktail may sound like the diet of Russian monks, ascetics and alcoholics. At Bompas & Parr we ran across the combo as the preferred drink of a sparkling curator at the Garage Centre of Contemporary Culture in Moscow. She is called Brittany Stewart. We were doing a fruit based artwork in the gallery. Initially we were appalled by the lack of decent flavour components, but found that the drink can be compelling.

A number of artisanal spirit producers are now making vodkas with the impurities left in for a nobler taste profile. Added water opens the spirit out so your palate can register the different notes – a little like watering a fine single malt.

We like to use seltzer. Bubbles within the glass can serve as flavour enhancers. They carry the volatile aromatics to olfactory receptors through the retro-nasal routes. So the vodka and soda becomes a drink of champions and connoisseurs, who really want to get to grips with the subtleties of flavour to be found in the vodka.

Sparkling water has a whole slew of romantic names from yesteryear you could use to gussie up your menu. Here are a few of the archaic terms that described what we now call soda water or pop – carbonade, oxygenated waters, gaseous alkaline, mephitic julep, marble waters, mephitic gas.

Incidentally a bubbly drink will be much more intoxicating than any flat libation. A team from the University of Surrey gave two groups of people flat and effervescent champagne containing the same levels of alcohol. Five minutes after drinking the glass the subjects who'd had the flat champagne only had 39 milligrams of alcohol in their blood while those on the sparkling champagne had a punchy 54 milligrams. With the bubbles carrying the alcohol to your mucus membranes it goes straight across the blood brain barrier and through your lungs and into the bloodstream bypassing your liver. Party on!

What's more the vodka and water combo is as close to the holy grail of the drinks industry – zero calorie alcohol, as is possible this side of Mars. To get a more advantageous calorie to intoxication ratio you would actually have to synthesise a (probably illegal) drug.

The combination of vodka and fruit has resulted in some of the most compelling drinks of the 20th century such as the Harvey Wallbanger, the Screwdriver, the Sea Breeze, the Sex on the Beach and the Woo Woo. In the 21st century the combination is set for a powerful comeback. Perhaps our Brittany is the drink to do this, encouraging people to offer ecstatic libations to the sky.

Ingredients
50ml 'Sipping' vodka or a decent quality vodka with some flavour characteristics of its own (from the freezer)
150ml soda water (from the fridge)
1 lemon wedge
1 lime wedge
1 orange wedge
1 maraschino cherry
Ice, to chill

To serve, fill a large wine glass with ice, add the vodka, top up with the soda and give it a whirl with a bar spoon. Jam in the fruit (all you can get your hands on) and serve with a straw.

The ratio of 1:3, vodka to soda means that this recipe can be scaled up with ease for party occasions, galas or making oversized drinks. Just mix it all up in a jug, pour over the ice-charged glasses and share with the crowd.

Offer ecstatic libations to the sky with The Brittany. The bubbles have an effect all of their own

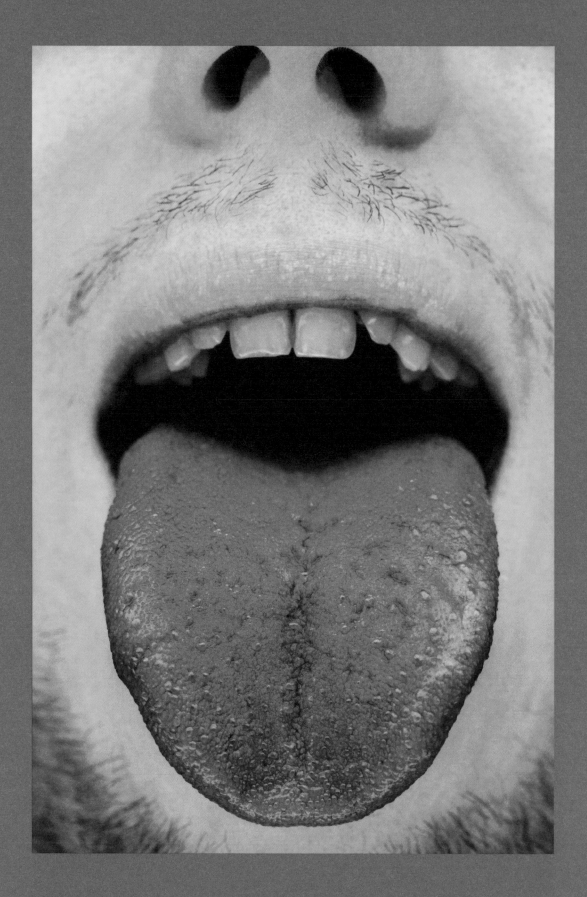

Use E133 to achieve the desired colour. Your choice, your refreshment

Blue Cocktails

By Sam Bompas. Photography by Nathan Pask

Here's a selection of blue cocktails coloured to please the eye and stain the tongue, they first appeared in *The Gourmand* issue 2. The Cyanopsia Fizz makes a particularly tasty companion as you reflect on Sam Jacob's Blue Raspberry essay on page 18.

Turquoise Negroni

Here's a cocktail that makes you genuflect and says – on your knees. It's based on cocktail legend Wayne Collin's white Negroni. According to Overfield it should taste even better dyed blue. Don't be shy about adding an E number to your Negroni. After all the red in the traditional Campari negroni comes from E120 otherwise known as carmine or cochineal. You may as well be honest about what's in the glass.

Ingredients – Serves 1
2 parts Tanqueray Gin
(the forward juniper botanicals help)
1 part Suze (a gentian liqueur)
1 part dry vermouth
E133 Brilliant Blue dye (to desired colour, your choice, your refreshment)

Pour all the ingredients into an old-fashioned glass over ice. Give a good stir and garnish with a twist of orange peel. Fend them off with a fistful of bar snacks and a cry of "get your own".

Cyanopsia Fizz

Cyanopsia's a hallucination where your vision is tinted blue. There are a few causes known to medical science. The first is having a cataract removed. The second and more common by far is a side effect of Viagra. This sparkling cocktail may bring on a blue vision all of its own.

Ingredients – Serves 7
1 punnet of raspberries
200ml blue Curaçao
1 bottle of pink champagne

Soak the raspberries overnight in the blue curaçao. Float in saucers of pink champagne to serve and watch them all flock.

Beyond the Waterfall

Here's a cocktail tribute to the bad old days of blue cocktailing. It's really about the monstrous garnish – a vast banana dolphin floating in your glass with a lurid maraschino cherry in its mouth.

Ingredients – Serves 1 but can be scaled up
2 parts vodka
1 part peach schnapps
1 part dry vermouth
3 drops of blue Curaçao

To garnish
1 banana (unpeeled)
1 maraschino cherry
(or any small fruit you can get your hands on)
2 whole cloves

It's best to start by making the garnish as this is quite a production. Start by taking a banana and cutting it in half. Take the end with the stalk and make an incision with your blade just under the stalk to make the dolphin's mouth. Hold it open by wedging the maraschino cherry (or lychee!) into the opening so it looks like the dolphin's playing with a ball. You may need to hold it in place with a cocktail stick. The final flourish is to make the dolphin's eyes using the two cloves.

Now you are ready to build the drink. Place all the liquid ingredients in a mixing glass filled with ice and stir with a mixing spoon. Now strain into a chilled martini glass and let your banana dolphin garnish frolic in the drink. You'll see this one in your dreams.

If garnishing with a maraschino cherry always opt for those with stalks. Your guests can make
like Audrey from *Twin Peaks* and use their tongues to tie it in a knot. There's always one

Carnival Punch

By Sam Bompas. Photography by Nathan Pask

Time flies when you're having rum. This is the first cocktail that Sam ever learnt how to brew up while working on the tropical island of Saint Kitts. There a friendly scaffolder taught him the singsong rhyme that outlines the desirable portions.

One of sour (acid – fresh lemon juice, lime juice)
Two of sweet (sugar syrup, honey, fructose syrup, etc.)
Three of strong (whatever alcohol you can get your hands on by rum is preferred)
Four of weak (any fruit juice you like)

He was also advised never to omit the following:
    Dash of bitters.
    Freshly grated nutmeg to serve.

The formula is relatively flexible so substitute in whatever fruit juices you like to drink. The key is an intermingling of many different fruit juices and alcohols to create something that will make all man with a bit of animal thrown in.

The recipe is still a winner. Each year we make litres and litres of the punch to take to the Notting Hill Carnival. This recipe is based on standard bottle sizes as you'll be making a lot and it's easier to scale at this size.

Enough for 4 thirsty people going to carnival or 22 regular drinkers.

Punch
1 pineapple (the flesh blitzed to pulp)
1 litre mango juice
(we use the cheap long-life fruit juices)
1 litre passion fruit juice
1 litre orange juice
3 granules of instant coffee
2 dashes of Angostura bitters
700ml dark rum (Meyers Rum would be appropriate)
350ml light overproof rum
100ml lime juice (freshly squeezed)
Grated nutmeg, to serve

Sugar syrup
100ml water
100g brown sugar

Begin by making the sugar syrup. For this recipe we use one made with brown sugar for the added flavour it brings to the drink. Boil the water in a pan, take it off the heat and stir the sugar into the liquid. Keep stirring until it has dissolved, then leave to cool.

Cut the flesh from the pineapple and blitz it in a food processor. Add the mango, passion fruit and orange juices and give it a stir to intermingle. Next, add the coffee granules (melted in a tiny splash of water) and the Angostura bitters and rums.

Now taste it. Do you like how it is shaping up? Add the lime juice and sugar syrup incrementally until the punch is balanced in terms of flavour and you are proud to serve it to many friends. If someone doesn't like what you've made, throw them to the lions.

Serve over ice in a tumbler with a straw (or more appropriately a solo party cup). Grate fresh nutmeg over to serve.

For us this is a quick and dirty party drink so we don't normally fancy it up with a garnish. If you'd like too you could add a maraschino cherry. It's not totally appropriate in the Caribbean drink but it adds excellent colour.

If you really want to sex it up, serve in a hollowed out pineapple that's been frozen ahead of service. Totally tropical!

WORKING UP TO YOUR FINALE:

ART INSTALLATIONS & CREATIVE PROJECTS

Fruit Salad The Artwork

By Jennifer Rubell
Photography by Martin Parr

This is a recipe for Fruit Salad, the artwork, which, though it might closely (or even exactly) resemble a fruit salad, occupies another sphere entirely.

It is an object which lives inside the history of art, occupying a fixed place on a continuous line that stretches from the Caves of Lascaux through the Venus of Willendorf, through Michelangelo and Leonardo, through Manet and Malevich, through Duchamp's Bicycle Wheel and Warhol, Marilyns, Elvises and Jackies, through the pimply 20 year-old kid who is currently in art school and who will eventually change the way we think about art forever, and on and on until the end of time. Fruit Salad, the artwork, however ephemeral it may be, will exist forever. (Fruit salad, the fruit salad, will be gone after breakfast.)

Ingredients
Conceptual Underpinning
Aesthetics
Originality
Intentionality
Context

Consider the meaning of a fruit salad, in any or all of the following contexts: historical, aesthetic, sociological, art-historical, personal. Begin to think about what it will mean for people to eat Fruit Salad, or what it will mean if you forbid them to touch it. Think about the fundamental differences between Fruit Salad and all previous works of art. Think about the similarities. Think about the problems caused to an art institution by the existence of Fruit Salad. Develop a language to talk about Fruit Salad, and write it down so you remember it.

Begin to conceptualise an object that contains and conveys all of your thoughts on fruit salad while at the same time being aesthetically compelling. Attempt to imagine a piece that is at once a rejection of all previous forms of art making and an acceptance of the pre-existing continuum of aesthetic and conceptual development.

Make something which has never been made before, which could only possibly be made by you at this very moment in time, and which, in its approach to the medium and subject, opens up a possibility of art making which did not exist prior to its conception.

Scrutinise the work, and make sure you stand behind every physical aspect of it. Each element of it must be entirely intentional, so that the viewer is certain that the work in question is the exact product of the artist's vision, and can be experienced, critiqued, and analyzed accordingly.

Determine where Fruit Salad will be shown. Particularly when creating works that can easily be mistaken for menu items, it is advisable to choose a traditional art viewing location: museum, kunsthalle, gallery, exhibition space or collector's private museum, etc. Please note the selected institution is not required to be complicit in the exhibition of the work.

UNITED ARAB EMIRATES. Dubai. DIFC Gulf Art Fair. 2007

GB. England. Henley on Thames. 1996

Tutti

•

Frutti

Fruit Cake The Installation

By Joana Vasconcelos

Issues of consumption and taste have always been right up my street, and one of the ways this has manifested itself in my work is through Fruit Cake, a concoction I am always happy to show off. Fresh like a summer breeze, this fun, giant cupcake is bound to be a hit among your friends. It's robust enough for an outdoor party and the happy colours and playful shapes bring back the sweetest childhood memories. Fruit Cake was especially conceived to look delicious (presentation is key!); eating it, however, may not be advisable.

Serves everyone

528 apple-shaped plastic sand moulds
188 pear-shaped plastic sand moulds
82 strawberry-shaped plastic sand moulds
456 pretzel-shaped plastic sand moulds
46 stainless steel hoops in different diameters*
(shop-bought is fine)
1254 stainless-steel rods
1254 stainless-steel rivets
2508 stainless-steel washers

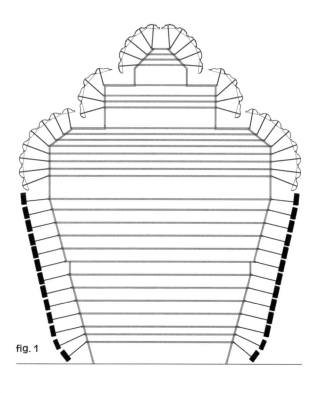

fig. 1

Start by building the stainless-steel structure, as this is what will hold Fruit Cake in place. Grab 13 large stainless-steel hoops and carefully weld them on to six vertical steel tubes, making sure they are equidistant. Repeat the process with five medium ones and with the five smaller ones, so to obtain a grid-like skeleton for your cupcake (fig. 1). Once the structure is done, weld the steel rods along the hoops; each of these rods will hold a single plastic sand mould, so don't separate them too much as you don't want the whole thing to become too see-through. Set aside.

Wash the fruit and pretzel-shaped sand moulds very carefully, as it's important they look nothing but squeaky clean. Using a drill, perforate the centre of each plastic mould – the ideal diameter for the holes is 4.25mm. Cover 13 of the bottom rows with pretzels, fix them on to the structure in the following order: put a rivet on the rod, then a washer, the mould and then another washer. This will prevent the rivet from deforming the mould. Repeat with the following seven rows using the apples, followed by five rows of pears and top it off with five rows of strawberries (you should end up with a sphere-shaped top layer). You will have most likely placed each sand mould a bit carelessly, which is fine, but in order to spruce up presentation you will have to twist each mould so that they are all lined up nicely in the exact same position. Exhibit.

Fruit Cake, 2011. Plastic sand moulds, stainless steel, 287 x Ø 250 cm
Courtesy Haunch of Venison, London. Photo: DMF, Lisbon/©Unidade Infinita Projectos

Tutti • Frutti

Tutti Frutti Chemicals: Jo Duck photographs Bompas & Parr's pyrotechnic trials exploring the colour potential of barium nitrate, boric acid, iron (III) hexacyanoferrate (II), strontium nitrate and zinc powder. All precautions were taken
Photography: Jo Duck

The Endless Fruit Salad

By Sissel Tolaas
Illustration by Tom Sewell

'We are so distant from the natural taste of things that we even start to prefer the artificial and we enjoy tasting and smelling the descriptions of the foods instead of the foods themselves'
– Marshal McLuhan

The chemical senses are the gatekeepers of the body. They provide information about substances in the outside world that influence our decisions on what to eat and drink and think. Our responses to tastes and smells appear to be hard-wired but they can be modified by experience. Much of what we like and dislike about tastes and smells is not genetic but learned. We are living in a world today where lemonade is made from artificial flavours and furniture polish is made from real lemons – and we can eat both.

I have always believed that food and eating are all about risky living. Because of the media hype and woefully inadequate information, too many people nowadays are deathly afraid of their food. But what does fear of food do to the digestive system? I am sure that an unhappy or suspicious stomach, constricted and uneasy with worry, cannot digest properly. And if digestion is poor, the whole body suffers. If you reject the food, ignore the customs, fear the religion, and avoid the people, you might as well stay home. Maybe a person's time would be as well spent raising food as raising money to buy food.

The next time you feel like complaining, remember that your rubbish disposal probably eats better than 30 per cent of the people in the world. And it is even more absurd that we live in an age when pizza gets to your home before the police, and believe it or not, Americans eat 75 acres of pizza a day. The science to feed people is worth at least as much as the science that teaches how to kill them.

I really love any taste if I can only get it by my nose.

1. Lay out these exotic fruits in front of you:

Durian	Monster Deliciosa	Dragon Fruit
Mangosteen	Jackfruit	Rambutan
Pepino	Cherimoya	
Cupuaqu	Breadfruit	

2. Taste the fruits carefully one by one. For each fruit, write down a description of its taste in terms of things that you know. (The descriptions will be different for each person depending on the individual's culture, background and geography.)

3. List the descriptions like the following:

Lychee	Pineapple	Skunk Spray
Grape	Apple	Raw Sewage
Kiwi Fruit	Strawberry	Almond
Pear	Chocolate	Gym Sock
Bubblegum	Melon	Rotten Onion
Banana	Lemon	Turpentine
Bread	Peach	

4. Get one of each item from the list you have just made. In this case you would need: one lychee, one grape, one kiwi, one pear, one bubblegum, one banana, one bread, one pineapple, one apple, one strawberry, one chocolate, one melon, one lemon, one peach, one skunk spray, one raw sewage, one almond, one gym sock, one rotten onion, one turpentine.

5. Taste the tastes carefully one by one. Describe each taste using adjectives and write them down for each item.

6. List the descriptions like the following:

Sweet	Juicy	Sulphuric
Floral	Acidic	Organic
Gritty	Spiky	Platonic
Bitter	Heavy	Synthetic
Pungent	Tropical	Milky
Rubbery	Sour	Fleshy
Creamy	Green	Fatty
Sodiac	Ashy	Nutty
Sweaty	Watery	Pungent
Buttery	Mealy	Cheesy
Fishy	Burnt	Salted
Tarty	Rotten	
Tangy	Musky	

7. Using the new list repeat steps 4 through 6 endlessly.

The Gherkin Chandelier
Poking Pickle Shaped Holes
In The Tissue Of Conventional
Ornamental Lighting

By Sam Bompas
Photography by Ann Charlott Ommedal

There's charm in a snappy luminous pickle. These sultans of savour come in the most lurid colours and are pre-done so that you are ready to feast. There's one idea for conquering gherkins that had been percolating in our studio's consciousness for a while. Challenged with creating a spectacular set piece for the recent Feast we knew the time had come to create the world's first gherkin chandelier.

It was a dangerous and ambitious project, but one you too can try if you are willing to risk electrocution. By passing a mains current through a gherkin it will fizz, spark and eventually illuminate, all the time heating the pickle to a frenzy, agitated by powerful electrical forces.

It's simple to achieve this effect on a single gherkin. Just take a normal plug and attach a steel rod to the live and neutral leads coming out of it. Jab the rods into each end of the gherkin and switch on the current. It won't disappoint. The prince of pickles works as a high resistance material, like the filament in a bulb glowing with a ghostly green light.

We spent a full week working with an electrical engineer and managed to establish that a small gherkin draws 300W while a large gherkin draws a huge 500W.

To scale up to a chandelier, we wired as many gherkins as we could get our hands on around a specially constructed chandelier frame. It was important to wire them in parallel so as not to decrease the voltage. In total, the chandelier drew so much power it could light an entire street and would have caused instant death to anyone who touched it.

We cast a haunting and eerie glow on the upturned faces of the assembled attendees of Feast. It was a total sensory assault. The power surging through the gherkins caused a little bit of pickle juice to sublimate and waft though the air. At the same time, the massed gherkins fizzed and spattered, generating the classic soundscape of electrocution.

If making a gherkin light yourself, take all precautions. Be careful not to hang on too long or you will totally cremate the pickles. Also, be advised that you might fuse your mains and there is a real danger of death, but the results will be worth it. Nothing beats the sensory stimulation of when gherkins collide with electricity.

The chandelier in action. Real danger of death and the waft of electrocuted pickle

Piñatas

By Thu Tran
Photography by Josef Kraska

I was racking my brain on this one. The more I thought about piñatas, the more I **overthought** piñatas. As fun as they seem, I have never truly desired to fill one up, only to smash it apart. I think piñatas look cool but being filled with cheap sweets that no one wants, seems so boring. If they were filled with gold nuggets and rubies, or foie gras and prawn eggs, or even boiling hot beef stew, then that would be way more exciting to me.

Even then, the act of being blindfolded, given a blunt stick and rendered dizzy before swinging your stick aimlessly at a cardboard animal covered in coloured tissue, while everyone points and laughs at you is, to say the least, a little humiliating. Not to mention having to squat down to pick all these cheap sweets off the ground. After the initial novelty of the idea of the piñata wore off, I completely lost interest.

However, through this thought process, I became interested in something a little more ridiculous. What I found interesting about the piñata concept is the act of being destructive and violent in order to reach your goal.

Here is what I intend to do. A big part of what I am proposing tis because my friend Jimmy Helvin recently gave me a rubbish bag full of colourful 30cm latex balloons and a blower (a mechanical balloon inflator). Immediately what came to mind was to fill my entire apartment up with the balloons, floor to ceiling, wall to wall, make myself a cactus suit, and run through the apartment, popping them all at once. This sounds like the funniest thing in the world to do, and would also be visually interesting. My apartment is small, (railway/shotgun style) so I could physically go through the whole apartment – all five rooms – in a straight path. I'm excited for the potential visuals here.

To make it even more exciting, I'd like to fill half the balloons up with helium so that ideally, it leaves a space about 30cm wide in the middle. It gives the option of 'superman-ing' through that gap. I'd also selectively fill up certain balloons with different treats to make it more of a treasure hunt. This experience combines the tradition of an Easter egg hunt with the smashing open of a piñata.

The balloons on the ceiling are filled with a variety of things. It's a fun game. They contain snack-sized bags of Doritos, loose pasta, pasta sauce, ribs, corn-on-the-cob. Dinner guests would walk through the balloonscape with plates and a glove that looks like a cactus. They can carefully choose which balloons they want to pop onto their plates. Some are trick balloons. They are filled with peanut butter and may splash open all over you. It's fun to give your dinner guests a truly unique experience.

The balloons on the floor are filled with dog and cat treats. They are for the pets. They are also alternatively filled with confetti.

This whole concept is a little absurdist and extremist, and less about the food itself, and more about the activity of getting your food.

Ingredients

1000 latex balloons
Mechanical balloon inflator
Helium tank
Scotch tape
Duct tape
Ribbon
Confetti
Cheap work gloves
Green tempera/acrylic paint
Needles
Hot glue

Edible ingredients

(I'm just listing my favourite foods here. They can be anything, not necessarily homemade either.

If you love McDonald's you can fill the balloons up with cheeseburgers and chips from there.)

Different types of pasta
Pasta sauces (marinara, vodka sauce, pesto, alfredo, etc.)
Ribs
Fried chicken
Small corn on the cobs
Crisps
Nacho cheese crisps
Cheese corn puffs
Peanut butter

Dog treats
Cat treats
Other pet treats

Definitely ask a friend or two help you set all this up. Have all your prepared food ready to go, and keep the human food separate from the pet snacks.

One person has to stretch the balloon open, the other puts the food inside the balloon. Once the food is inside, the balloon is inflated with the blower (or with the breath of your mouth) and tied off accordingly.

This all seems like it might take a long time, but I think you only need to fill up about 50 balloons or so. The remaining 950 can just be filled with air or confetti. You can pass the time during the activity by gossiping or playing loud music. The human food hangs on the ceiling, the pet food stays on the ground.

Stuff your apartment with treat filled balloons and begin making the cactus suit

Fruit Music Mixtape

By Mike Gabel of Hot Breath Karaoke
Photography by Beth Evans

A CORNUCOPIA
BONUS!
OF SOUND AND SAVOUR

"A table, a chair, a bowl of fruit and a violin; what else does a man need to be happy?" – Albert Einstein

I feel this quote eloquently demonstrates a higher understanding of something profound and life affirming, the pleasures derived from the simple combination of fruit and music. Is it possible that Einstein's theory of relativity was devised whist listening to Brahms and enjoying some fresh melon? Does $E=MC^2$ actually mean "Enjoyment = Music times cantaloupe squared?" Sit down, pop on your headphones and enjoy this playlist specifically chosen to heighten your fruit salad experience.

Banana **Boy**
Eden Ahbez

Our first spoonful is a bit of banana themed exotica from 1950's proto hippie, Eden Ahbez. Famous for writing Nat King Cole's no. 1 hit Nature Boy, Eden allegedly lived under the L in the Hollywood sign, ate nothing but fruit and sadly left the world with only one album, the enchanting easy listening classic, Eden's Island. It's a bit like Robinson Crusoe meets Jack Kerouac on the set of South Pacific and if you close your eyes you can almost imagine yourself drifting away, the sweet smell of bananas and hibiscus flowers filling your nose as Eden sits crossed legged scribbling poetry on the banana skins piled beneath your hammock. The next time you eat a banana, hold it to your ear and you might just hear Nature Boy.

Pineapple **Princess**
Annette Funicello

The pineapple, in my opinion, is the crown jewel of any fruit salad bowl. I will never forget a family holiday back in the 80's where my father (who happens to have a peculiar fondness for heavy industry as tourism) booked us on a tour of the Dole pineapple processing plant in Hawaii. I suppose he thought it would be like visiting Willy Wonka's chocolate factory. Well, it wasn't, but they did have drinking fountains that spouted pineapple juice which blew my 10 year old mind and subsequently blew my 10 year old stomach. Musically our pineapple fountain comes from squeaky clean ex-Mickey Mouseketeer, Annette Funicello with Pineapple Princess .

Apples, Peaches **and Cherries**
The Smothers Brothers

Our next two tracks take us into the enthralling world of the fruit vendor. First off, The Smothers Brothers tell us about a man, seemingly so enamoured with a young fruit seller and her wares that he purchases all of her stock, tracks her down and impregnates her 10 times. Apparently the moral of the story is to avoid people who sell things door to door, but maybe it's actually a cautionary tale about fruit as a powerful aphrodisiac.

Fruitman
Kool & The Gang

Our second seller song comes from Kool & The Gang with Fruitman, a song which chronicles the highly anticipated arrival of the neighbourhood fruit van through the medium of easy going funk. And luckily for us, it exists simply because at some point in 1974, The Gang were sat around a table and Kool said: "You know what this album needs? More songs about fruit." Thanks, Kool.

The Mango **Song**
Marty Robbins

I read recently that the mango is the most eaten fruit in the world. Well they certainly must be popular if they managed to get a country crooner like Marty Robbins to record a song that wasn't about whisky, a truck or a broken heart. It kind of makes me miss the good old days when everybody put out a fruit themed calypso record.

The Watermelon Song
Tennessee Ernie Ford

And while we are on the subject of country singers singing about fruit, let's move on to Tennessee Ernie Ford and The Watermelon Song. Ernie loves his pork chops, corn bread and black eyed peas like most southern gentleman do, but given half the chance he would gladly trade them in for a big ol' slice of watermelon. He even goes so far as to say he prefers watermelon to the affections of his missus. I certainly hope nobody finds a watermelon in Ernie's garden with some holes in it.

Peaches – *The Presidents of the Unites States of America*

If you were a peach farmer in 1995 who decided after a lacklustre season to switch to growing apples in 1996, you probably really, really wished you had stuck it out with the peaches for another year. Hearing this song on the radio every day probably didn't help matters either.

Licky Licky
Crispy

I'm not sure what the Danish sprinkled on their fruit salad in the 90's , but it inspired a bunch of them to form a band called Crispy and record some dance floor fluff about exotic fruit called Licky Licky. I absolutely love the song but I have a few questions. Like why on Earth would you call your band Crispy? And why does kiwi make you scream? Oh yeah, and what is a mango shot and where can I get one? And most importantly how can I get this song out of my head because it's literally driving me bananas?

Da Coconut Nut
Smokey Mountain

The Philippines is the world's top producer of the coconut. It also happens to be the world's top producer of boy bands named after landfills. Smokey Mountain was the name of Manila's home to over two million metric tons of waste and also served as the namesake for Manila's number one musical proponents of the coconut tree and its many uses. I think the lyrics of this song were lifted directly from a coconut tree information leaflet.

Fresh Fruit
Procol Harum

Our final bite into this musical fruit salad comes from symphonic rockers Procol Harum, who decide here to give the symphony the day off for this lazy ode to the virtues of fresh fruit. Where better to finish than with a song that tells us in that 1970's back to nature kind of way that "Fruit's the finest food on earth". It sounds like the tan you get after picking fruit all day in dungarees with no shirt. Does fruit taste better in stereo? I think so.

Tutti Frutti Italian style – in Italy hundreds and thousands are known as tutti frutti.
Presented on a pig's head they make for a meaty and affordable party decoration

Salute

Finally a toast to all those who have made this fruit adventure possible. Your expertise and creativity has been absolutely righteous. A hearty cheer for all those who contributed to Tutti Frutti. We salute you with overflowing cornucopias of fruit:

Writing and recipes
Nicola Twilley
Anna Murray of Patternity
Sam Jacob of FAT
Carla Henriques of Hawksmoor
Lily Vanilli
Yinka Shonibare, MBE
Elena Arzak of Arzak
Caitlin Williams Freeman
Alexis Gauthier of Gauthier Soho
Michael Cirino of a razor, a shiny knife
Joseph Wagenaar of
Andaz Liverpool Street
Florence Knight
Heather Ring of Wayward Plants
Justin Piers Gellatly of St John
Amanda Walker of
Peyton & Byrne at Kew
Thor Bergquist of ECC
Henrietta Lovell of
the Rare Tea Company
Jennifer Rubell
Joana Vasconcelos
Sissel Tolaas
Thu Tran
Mike Gabel of Hot Breath Karaoke

Photography, illustration and styling
Andrew Stellitano
Nathan Pask
Herbarium, Library, Art & Archives at the Royal Botanic Gardens, Kew
Emma Rios
José López
Caitlin Williams Freeman
Noah Kalina
Beth Evans
Ann Charlott Ommedal
Martin Parr
Joana Vasconcelos
Tom Sewell
Josef Kraska

Katy Pople
Olivia French
Jo Duck
Justin Ramsden
Andras Bartok
Nora Lidgus

Editing
Kathy Steer
Philippa Warr

Design and Art Direction
Inventory Studio
Design, Matt Bucknall at
Inventory Studio

And from Bompas & Parr
Sam Bompas
Harry Parr
Ann Charlott Ommedal
Olivia Bennett
Beth Adams
Abi Shapiro

Special thanks
Marina Tweed of *The Gourmand*
Brittany Stewart of Garage Centre of Contemporary Culture
Kit Neale for the Tutti Frutti apron on page 4
Herbarium, Library, Art & Archives at the Royal Botanic Gardens, Kew

First published in the United Kingdom in 2013 by Bompas & Parr Editions, London SE1 1ES.

ISBN: 978-0-9576477-0-1

Printed and bound by Push Print

www.bompasandparr.com

Text Credits
Bompas & Parr would like to thank the following for providing essays and recipes for Tutti Frutti:

©: pp. 7–13: Nicola Twilley, pp. 14–16: Anna Murray, pp. 18–20: Sam Jacob, pp. 22–29: Beth Adams, p. 33: Carla Henriques, p. 34: Lily Vanilli, pp. 34,36: Joseph Wagenaar, pp. 36–37,39–40: Abi Shapiro, p. 37: Yinka Shonibare, p. 39: Caitlin Williams Freeman, pp. 40,42: Michael Cirino, p. 43: Alexis Gauthier, pp. 46,49,53,55–56: Olivia Bennett, p. 45: Elena Arzak, pp. 61–62: Florence Knight, pp. 63,65: Heather Ring, pp. 68,70: Justin Piers Gellatly, p. 73: Amanda Walker, p. 75: Henrietta Lovell, pp. 75–76: Thor Bergquist, p. 83: Jennifer Rubell, p. 86: Joana Vasconcelos, p. 90: Sissel Tolaas, p. 94: Thu Tran, pp. 97–98: Mike Gabel, pp. 5, 31,51,56–61,62, 67–68,71,73,76–81,92,100: Bompas & Parr

Picture Credits
Bompas & Parr would like to thank the following for providing photographs/illustrations for Tutti Frutti:

©: Cover and endpapers: Andrew Stellitano, Fruit stickers pp. 2,3,6, 32,52,66,74,82,96,100: Inventory Studio, pp. 4,35,47,48,72,77,78,80,: Nathan Pask Photography, pp. 7,8,12: Nicola Twilley, pp. 16–17: Katy Pople, pp. 23–29: Herbarium, Library, Art & Archives at the Royal Botanic Gardens, Kew. p. 30: Emma Rios, p. 38: Caitlin Williams Freeman, p. 41: Noah Kalina, p. 43: Alexis Gauthier, p. 44: José López, pp. 50,99: Beth Evans, pp. 54,57,64,93: Ann Charlott Ommedal, pp. 84–85: Martin Parr/Magnum Photos, p. 86: Joana Vasconcelos, p. 87: DMF, Lisbon/Unidade Infinita Projectos, p. 91: Tom Sewell, p. 95: Josef Kraska, pp. 88–89: Jo Duck

SALUTE

#0–100